Critters of Massachusetts Pocket Guide

Produced in cooperation with Wildlife Forever

by Ann E. McCarthy, Director of Education

Adventure Publications, Inc.
Cambridge, Minnesota

Dedication

To Connor, Luke, Leanne and Erin in memory of th Grandpa Fulton of East Weymouth who loved canoeing a ice-skating on Elias' Pond and to the Scott Family who tr treasure the natural beauty of Massachusetts.

– Ann E. McCar

Research and Editorial Assistance: David A. Frederick

Technical Editor: Ellie Horwitz, Chief, Information & Education, MassWildlife

Cover, interior design and illustrations: Jonathan Norberg

Photo Credits: **Dominique Braud:** 68 (perching) **Bill Byrn** 94, 106, 110 **Mary Clay:** 28, 74 **Brian Collins:** 88 (femal 100 (female) **Sharon Cummings:** 18, 96 **E. R. Degginger:** 4 70, 76 **Dan Dempster:** 82 (female) **Dudley Edmondson:** 2 68 (soaring) **John Gerlach:** 44 **Richard Haug:** 36 **Ada Jones:** 54, 56 (female), 82 (male) **Rolf Kopfle:** 86 **Bill Le** 14 **Bill Marchel:** 30, 52 (both) **Maslowski Wildl Productions:** 20, 32, 34, 40, 50, 84, 98 **Gary Meszaros:** **John Mielcarek:** 24, 48, 102 **Larry Mishkar:** 108 **Sk Moody:** 12, 26, 56 (male), 78, 90, 104 **Alan Nelson:** 1 46, 64 **Stan Osolinski:** 60 **John Pennoyer:** 88 (male) **R Planck:** 92 **Fritz Polking:** 80 **Carl R. Sams II:** 66, 72 **St Tekiela:** 58, 62, 100 (male)

Third Printing

Published by Adventure Publications, Inc.
820 Cleveland Street South
Cambridge, MN 55008
1-800-678-7006
www.adventurepublications.net

Printed in China
ISBN-10: 1-885061-29-3
ISBN-13: 978-1-885061-29-4

FOREWORD

by Secretary Bob Durand, Executive Office of Environmental Affairs

Massachusetts is home to an amazing diversity of plants, animals and habitats. From the waters off Cape Cod to the mountains of the Berkshires, from pristine forests to urban parks, this wildlife heritage belongs to all the people of the Commonwealth.

As chief steward of the environment, I work through our public agencies to secure open space and conserve the biodiversity of the state. One of the best tools we have to protect our environment is a citizenry that cares about wildlife and the other natural resources that make Massachusetts an exceptional place to live. To encourage people to develop a personal connection to their environment, we have initiated annual "BioDiversity Days" during which children and adults—novices through experts—observe and record the many plants and animals around them.

When I meet groups of young people I often ask how many have spent time outdoors during the week. Too many spend all of their free hours indoors, and do not take the opportunity to explore the outdoors. They are losing out on a vital and enjoyable learning experience.

This booklet can help teachers take their students outdoors, and encourage youngsters (and others) who would like to get acquainted with our most common wildlife species. It can be the first step toward a lifetime of outdoor enjoyment.

Very truly yours,

Bob Durand

Bob Durand
Secretary, Executive Office
of Environmental Affairs

Table of Contents

About Wildlife Forever

Wildlife Forever is a nonprofit conservation organization de icated to conserving America's wildlife heritage throu education, preservation of habitat and management of fi and wildlife. Working at the grassroots level, Wildlife Forev has completed conservation projects in all 50 states. Wildl Forever's innovative outreach programs include the Wildl Forever State-Fish Art Project and the Theodore Roosev Conservation Alliance.

Cry of the Wild

The "cry of the wild" can still be heard across this great land. I have heard the bugle of an elk amid the foothills of the western plains...the shrill of a bald eagle along the banks of the mighty Mississippi...the roar of a brown bear on windswept tundra...the thunder of migrating waterfowl on coasta shores...the gobble of a wild turkey among eastern hardwoods and the haunting cry of a sandhill crane in the wetlands of the Central Flyway. America is truly blessed–a land rich in natural resources. This legacy must be preserved.

I hope this book will provide you with an insight to the many wonders of the natural world and serve as a stepping-stone to the great outdoors.

Yours for wildlife...forever,

Douglas H. Grann
President & CEO,
Wildlife Forever

To learn more contact us a
763-253-0222, 2700
Freeway Blvd., Ste. 1000,
Brooklyn Center, MN 554
or check out our website a
www.wildlifeforever.org.

INTRODUCTION

by Director Wayne F. MacCallum, MassWildlife

More than 650 species of wild mammals, birds, reptiles, amphibians and fish live in Massachusetts, and we have barely begun to tally the incredible number of insects and other invertebrates.

MassWildlife is dedicated to conserving and enhancing this rich diversity of wildlife by protecting and managing all our native species and the habitat on which they depend. We have, through careful management, restored populations of Black Bear, White-tailed Deer, Beaver, Wild Turkey, Peregrine Falcon and Bald Eagle. Each time an animal is removed from the list of threatened species, it is another step toward a better, healthier environment.

Since MassWildlife began in 1866, we have cleaned up our rivers and restored many of our fisheries resources, the percentage of woodland habitat has increased markedly, and many wildlife populations are thriving as never before.

Our challenge now is to maintain all wildlife populations in good health and keep them in balance with their environment and with people. This is a huge responsibility, but we can meet it with the help of citizens who understand the needs and management of wildlife populations.

Few things are more rewarding than discovering wildlife and learning about its habits and behaviors. Fewer still are more important than ensuring that the wildlife we have today will be there for future generations. That is our commitment; that is why we are MassWildlife.

Wayne F. MacCallum

Wayne F. MacCallum
Director, MassWildlife

FACTS
About Massachusetts

Massachusetts. The name comes from the Massachuset Indian people and means "great hill." The natural landscape of an expansive coastline, islands, inlets and bays have contributed greatly to the character, tradition and culture of Massachusetts.

The Atlantic Ocean provides a rich bounty including scallops, clams, lobster, crab, perch, flounder, mackerel, haddock and cod. Fishing is the oldest industry in the state.

Just beyond the beaches, sand dunes and salt-marsh grasses of the coast are stands of pitch pines and scrub oaks. Proceeding west, the land becomes hilly and covered with hardwoods including birch, maple, ash, beech and oak. Roughly 2/3 of the state is forested. Violets, trillium and ferns dot the forest floor. Rivers and streams including the Merrimac, Mystic and Concord cut through the hills and valleys. The Berkshire Hills and Taconic Mountains dominate western Massachusetts.

Shores, woodlands, alpine meadows, rivers and streams provide tremendous habitat diversity for wildlife. National Wildlife Refuges and protected state and private lands offer an amazing diversity of habitats and wildlife.

Bay Staters enjoy the natural beauty of more than 285,000 acres of state forests and parks and over 100,000 acres of Wildlife Management Areas. Massachusetts may be small in size, but it is jam-packed with natural beauty and outdoor adventures just waiting for people to enjoy.

State Bird:
Black-capped Chickadee

State Fish:
Cod

State Gem:
Rhodonite

State Marine Mammal:
Right Whale

State Nicknames:
Old Colony State, Bay State

State Flower:
Mayflower

State Tree:
American Elm

State Mineral:
Babingtonite

State Insect:
Ladybug

How to Use This Guide

While this book is not intended as a field guide (we dor want anyone getting too close to a bear trying to identify i species!), it is intended to be a great reference for informa tion on some of the fascinating animals that we loosely ca the "critters" of Massachusetts. We think that the mo information people have about wildlife and their needs, th more we can do to conserve this wonderful part of our na ural world.

Notes About Icons

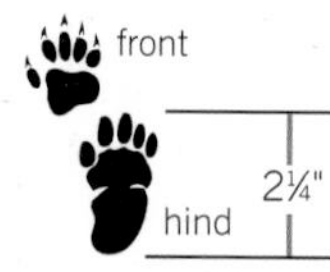

In the mammal section, the track one foot is included near the botto right of the page. The size, from top bottom is included beside it. Whe appropriate, the front and hind print a included with the front placed at the to of the oval, and the hind at the bottom. Note that for som animals such as the cottontail, you will find that in a set tracks, the hind print actually appears ahead of the fron This will be apparent in the layout of the tracks as shown the right margin. While the sizes of the individual tracks ar relative to each other, the pattern of tracks is not. We woul have needed a very large page to accommodate the moos tracks compared to the chipmunk!

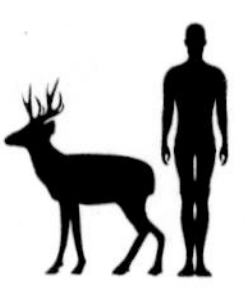

The animal/person silhouette on the bo tom left of the mammal pages is to sho the relative size of the animal compare to an average-sized adult. Sometime it's easier to judge comparisons tha actual measurements.

nocturnal (active at night)

diurnal (active during day)

crepuscular (most active at dawn and dusk)

Zzz *hibernator/deep sleeper* (dormant during winter)

ne yellow symbols depicting the sun, moon or the sun on e horizon indicate whether the animal is nocturnal, diurnal crepuscular. While you may see these animals at other nes, they are most active during the periods shown. The llow Zzzs indicate whether or not the animal hibernates. ome critters are true hibernators, which means their body ocesses slow down a great deal and they require very little nergy to survive the winter. Other critters are deep sleepers, nd their body processes slow down only a little and they equire greater amounts of energy to survive the winter.

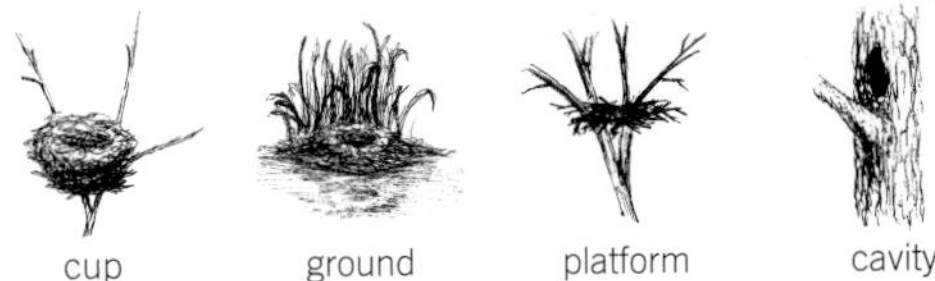

n the bird pages, the nest type is shown at the bottom ght. This indicates whether the bird builds a cup-type nest, ground nest, a platform nest or a cavity nest.

n the Lifelist on page 112, place a check by each mammal r bird you've seen, whether in your backyard or at the zoo.

DID YOU KNOW...? The bat is the only mammal capable of flight. It uses echolocation (sound waves) to detect and catch insects. It is capable of catching 600 moths in one hour and thousands of mosquitoes in a single night. Each fall, as temperatures begin to drop and the numbers of insects decline, they migrate to favorite hibernation sites, which include caves and mines. They return to breeding sites in late spring.

Bat, Little Brown

Myotis lucifugus

Size: body 3-4½" long with a 1½" forearm; 8-9" wingspan; weighs ¼-⅓ oz.

Habitat: in summer, wooded areas near water; in winter they hibernate in caves and mines

Range: throughout Massachusetts; uncommon on Nantucket

Food: flying insects including midges, mosquitoes, beetles and moths

Mating: prior to hibernation each fall; gestation of 60 days (after a delayed period of 7 months after mating)

est Site: colonize and roost in groups in attics and other buildings, tree cavities and caves

Young: one pup is born, commonly in maternity colonies of 300-600 females; dark brown in color, they weigh 30% of adult and nurse for approximately 4 weeks; able to fly at 3 weeks

edators: Screech-Owl, raccoon, domestic cat and snake

Tracks: none

scription: The little brown bat has a coat of silky cinna-
on-buff to dark brown hair, with pale gray undersides and
nd-like wings. It skims the water's surface where it catches
sects at a rate of one every eight seconds.

no tracks

DID YOU KNOW...? The black bear is the largest carnivore in New England. It is an excellent climber and can run at speeds of 25 mph. In the winter, the black bear spends up to three months in its den, living off its stored body fat. Cubs are born in the winter while the female is in the den. The black bear loves honey and any other sweet food. It sometimes forages in suburban and agricultural areas.

diurnal Zzz *deep sleeper*

Bear, Black

Ursus americanus

Size: body 4½-5' long; stands 2-3' high at shoulder; female weighs 100-250 lbs., male weighs 150-350 lbs.

Habitat: forests mixed with open areas and wetlands

Range: central and western Massachusetts

Food: nuts, grasses, tubers, fruit, berries and insects; will also raid bird feeders, beehives and trash cans

Mating: June to July; gestation of about 60 days (after a delayed period of 5 months after mating)

Den: located in brush piles, rock crevices, hollow logs, under fallen trees or beneath uprooted trees

Young: cubs, usually twins, born blind and hairless with pinkish skin; 8" long; 8 oz.; eyes open at 40 days; cubs nurse and remain in den until spring; independent at 18 months

redators: none in Massachusetts

Tracks: tracks show 5 toes, claw marks and a large heel pad

escription: The black bear's fur is usually black with a own muzzle and occasionally a small white chest patch. has a small, narrow head with thick rounded ears. It arks trees by clawing and ripping off bark.

4"

7-9"

DID YOU KNOW...? A beaver can chew down hundreds of trees each year. One family of beavers may consume as much as a ton (2,000 lbs.) of bark in a single winter. To maintain water levels, beavers build dams averaging 100' long. The beaver is especially adapted to life in water with waterproof fur, webbed hind feet, goggle-like eyelids and valves that keep water out of its nose and ears. It's able to hold its breath for 15 minutes.

nocturnal crepuscular

BEAVER

Castor canadensis

Size: body 20-25" long; tail 15" long, 7" wide; weighs 30-60 lbs.

Habitat: fresh water streams, rivers, ponds or lakes bordered by woodlands

Range: northeast, central and western Massachusetts

Food: in spring and summer, leaves, buds, twigs, ferns, stems and roots of aquatic plants; in fall and winter, bark of hardwood trees that they have cached

Mating: mid-January to mid-March; gestation of 100-110 days

Den: lodge; dome-shaped structure, 5-6' tall, 20-30' wide, with underwater entrance

Young: 2-6 kits born with thick dark fur; 1 lb. each; able to swim soon after birth but remain inside den for 6 weeks; nurse for 8-10 weeks; fully independent at 20 months

redators: coyote and bobcat

Tracks: small front prints and webbed hind prints often erased by tail as it drags behind

escription: The beaver is a large rodent with prominent ange teeth, and a large, flat, paddle-shaped tail. Look r tree cuttings near the shoreline and mud mounds arked with scent. Listen for tail slaps on the water.

6"

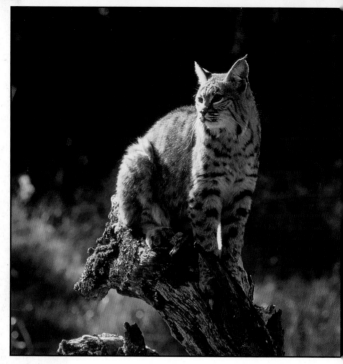

DID YOU KNOW...? Found only in North America, and the most common wildcat in Massachusetts, the bobcat is named for its stubby, bobbed tail. It can leap 7-10' in a single bound. An excellent climber, it uses trees for resting, observation and protection. It can travel 3-7 miles for a hunt and stores uneaten food under vegetation.

nocturnal *crepuscular*

BOBCAT

Lynx rufus

Size: body 26-36" long; tail 4-7" long; stands 20-30" high at shoulder; weighs 15-40 lbs.

Habitat: mixed forests with brushy understory and rocky ledges

Range: northeast, central and western Massachusetts

Food: rabbits, mice, squirrels, muskrats, birds and eggs, snakes, fish, deer and carrion (remains of dead animals)

Mating: late February to March; gestation of 50-70 days

Den: rock crevices, under windfalls, brush piles or in hollow logs

Young: 2-3 kittens born blind; 10" long; 12 oz. each; eyes open a few days after birth; kittens nurse for 8 weeks; begin to eat meat at 4 weeks; fully independent at 5 months

redators: young attacked by Great Horned Owl

Tracks: large prints show 4 toes and no claw marks

escription: The bobcat has a yellowish gray coat with ddish brown streaks and a sprinkling of black and a soft eige underside. It is mostly gray during winter months. gns may include scratch marks on trees and shredded ark.

2"

mammals

DID YOU KNOW...? The Eastern chipmunk is able to run 15 feet per second. It uses its outsized cheek pouches to store and carry food. Frost causes it to head for its den, where it spends a few weeks to several months in a deep sleep. It wakes frequently to eat stored food.

diurnal Zzz *deep sleeper*

Chipmunk, Eastern

Tamias striatus

Size: body 3-5" long; tail 3-4" long; weighs 2½-4½ oz.

Habitat: wooded and brushy areas with loose soil; also in suburban areas with lots of cover such as decaying logs, rock piles and stone walls

Range: throughout Massachusetts except Nantucket

Food: nuts, buds, fruit, seeds, insects, bird eggs, fungi, bulbs and acorns

Mating: February to April and June to July; gestation of 31 days

Den: part of an underground tunnel system with several chambers; entrance is 1½" across; often found under rock piles, brush piles and tangled roots

Young: 1-8 young born blind and hairless; 0.1 oz.; 2 litters per year; fuzzy coat appears at 2 weeks; eyes open at 4 weeks; fully independent at 8 weeks

redators: coyote, bobcat, fox, hawk, owl, weasel, snake and domestic cat

Tracks: difficult to find because of small size; front feet show 4 toes, hind feet show 5

escription: The Eastern chipmunk is reddish brown ith 5 dark stripes alternating with gray; lighter underde. It leaves a trail of chewed nutshells. Its call is a uick "chip-chip-chip."

⅝"

1"

DID YOU KNOW...? Burrows provide winter cover for the cottontail. A group of burrows is called a warren. The cottontail has great eyesight and speed, as well as protective coloring. It is a very important prey species in North America.

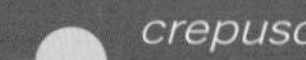

Cottontail, Eastern

Sylvilagus floridanus

Size: body 14-18" long; tail 2" long; weighs 2-4 lbs.

Habitat: fields and thickets; may live in woodchuck holes

Range: throughout Massachusetts

Food: in summer, tender grasses, herbs and garden crops; in winter, bark, twigs and buds of shrubs or young trees; eats own scat for added food value

Mating: March to August; gestation of 28 days

Nest Site: 5" deep depression (burrow) lined with plant material and fur; usually found in meadows or at the base of trees

Young: 4-7 young born hairless and blind; 4" long; 1 oz. each; 3-4 litters per year; eyes open at 1 week; young nurse for 4 weeks; fully independent at 5 weeks

Predators: coyote, fox, domestic dog and cat, bobcat, hawk and owl

Tracks: both front and hind show 4 toes, but pads aren't clear because of thick fur on the feet

Description: The cottontail is a grayish brown rabbit with rusty colored fur behind its ears. It has a fluffy, cottony white tail.

1"

3½"

DID YOU KNOW...? Unique to North America, the coyote is portrayed as a clever creature in certain Native American folklore. It's capable of running at speeds of more than 30 mph. Its distinct howl, coupled with short high-pitched yelps can often be heard, sometimes as far away as 3 miles. Coyotes can sometimes be spotted in suburban areas.

nocturnal crepuscular

Coyote, Eastern

Canis latrans

Size: body 32-40" long; tail 12-15" long; stands 15-20" high at shoulder; weighs 30-40 lbs.

Habitat: woodlands, grasslands, brushy fields and suburban areas

Range: throughout Massachusetts except Martha's Vineyard and Nantucket

Food: mice, squirrels, rabbits and other small mammals, birds, frogs, snakes, fish, fruits, berries, sometimes deer, and carrion (remains of dead animals); stores uneaten food under leaves and soil

Mating: January to March; gestation of 58-63 days

Den: usually underground; will dig its own or enlarge an abandoned den

Young: 5-10 pups born blind and grayish; 8 oz. each; eyes open at 8-14 days; pups nurse for several weeks; later both adults feed pups regurgitated food; independent at 6-9 months

'redators: none in Massachusetts

Tracks: similar to medium-sized dog tracks; show 4 toes, claw marks and a rear pad

'escription: Coyotes are usually gray but can vary from ;ht yellow brown to dark red or black. It has longer black-oped fur on its shoulders and a bushy black-tipped tail.

2½"

DID YOU KNOW...? When alarmed, the white-tailed deer raises its tail resembling a white flag. It can run up to 35-40 mph. During the breeding season, males make marks (rubs) on sapling trees with their antlers to make rival males aware of their presence. Males spar with each other over females.

crepuscular

Deer, White-tailed

Odocoileus virginianus

Size: body 4-6' long; tail 6-13" long; stands 2-3' high at shoulder; male weighs 100-300 lbs., female weighs 85-130 lbs.

Habitat: woodlands, wetlands, fields and brushy areas

Range: throughout Massachusetts

Food: leaves, stems, buds, grasses, mushrooms, wildflowers, crops, acorns and beechnuts

Mating: October to December; 7 months gestation; males make scrapes, which are patches of muddy ground where they urinate to attract females

Bedding Site: shallow depressions in hidden areas

Young: 1-3 fawns born with white spots for camouflage; spots remain for 3-4 months; 8 lbs. each; fawns nurse for several months; fully independent at 1 year

·edators: coyote, bobcat and domestic dog

Tracks: narrow, heart-shaped with split hoof

·escription: White-tailed deer have a reddish brown coat ·summer, grayish brown in winter. In spring, males grow ·ward-facing antlers that are shed in winter.

3"

DID YOU KNOW...? The fisher is one of the few predators of the porcupine. It strikes the porcupine's face and then flips it over, exposing its vulnerable belly. Fishers can be seen in suburban areas.

nocturnal

Fisher

Martes pennanti

Size: body 20-31" long; tail 10-16" long; weighs 4-15 lbs.; males twice as large as females

Habitat: mixed forests; favors wetlands

Range: throughout Massachusetts except Cape Cod, Martha's Vineyard and Nantucket

Food: snowshoe hare, mice, squirrels, porcupine, chipmunks, muskrat, raccoon, frogs, carrion (remains of dead animals), insects, berries and nuts

Mating: February to March; gestation of 30 days (after a delayed period of 9-10 months after mating)

Den: hollow tree, log, or rock crevice

Young: 1-5 kits born blind and hairless; 1 oz.; eyes open at 7 weeks; nurse for 10 weeks; kits are independent at 6 months

redators: none in Massachusetts

Tracks: cat-like; show 5 toes and C-shaped pad measuring 2-4" in length

escription: Fishers have thick, glossy fur that is dark ·own. The tips of the hairs on the head and shoulders are ·ay. They occupy a range of 5-8 square miles.

2-4"

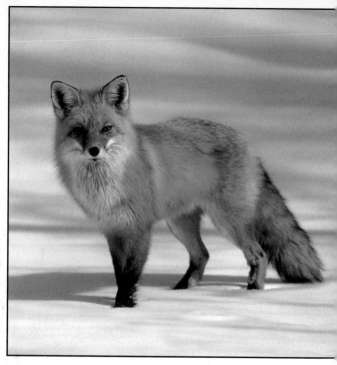

DID YOU KNOW...? The red fox can leap 15' in a single bound. The fox can run up to 30 mph and is an excellent swimmer. It stores uneaten food under leaf litter or snow marked with urine, usually near the den entrance.

nocturnal crepuscular

Fox, Red

Vulpes vulpes

Size: body 20-40" long; tail 14-16" long; stands 14-16" high at shoulder; weighs 8-15 lbs.

Habitat: forests, fields and suburban areas

Range: throughout Massachusetts except Martha's Vineyard and Nantucket

Food: insects, fruit, berries, birds, frogs, turtle eggs, mice, rabbits and carrion (remains of dead animals)

Mating: mid-January to late February; gestation of 52 days

Den: often found in hilly areas, in tree roots, under woodpiles and in abandoned woodchuck burrows; entrance is 8-15" across

Young: 4 to 5 kits born charcoal gray; 3-8 oz.; young nurse for 10 weeks, later both adults feed them regurgitated food; independent at 7 months

redators: coyote and bobcat

Tracks: small dog-like tracks follow a straight line; claws show

escription: The red fox shows several color variations om rusty red to black, silver and dark brown, all with hite undersides. It has black legs and a white-tipped il.

2¼"

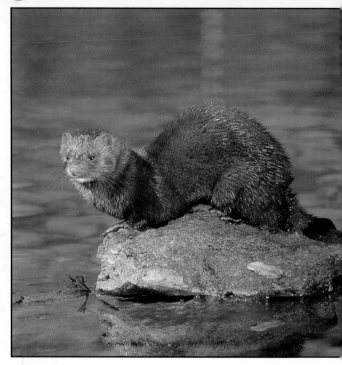

DID YOU KNOW...? In spite of its small size, the mink is an aggressive predator. It commonly kills prey in their burrows. The mink may dig its own den, but it often takes over abandoned muskrat burrows and beaver lodges. It seldom stays in its den for long periods.

nocturnal

Mink

Mustela vison

Size: body 12-22" long; tail 6-9" long; weighs 1½-4½ lbs.

Habitat: stream banks, lakeshores and marshes

Range: throughout Massachusetts except Nantucket and perhaps Martha's Vineyard

Food: fish, frogs, mice, ducks, eggs, insects, snakes, crayfish, chipmunks, rabbits, muskrats and carrion (remains of dead animals)

Mating: late February to early April; gestation of 28–32 days (after a delayed period of 12-43 days after mating)

Den: lined with fur and grass; usually near waterways, often under tree roots or in abandoned burrows of muskrat or beaver

Young: 2-10 kits born blind and covered with fine white fur; 1-2" long weighing 1 oz.; eyes open at 25 days; nurse for 5 weeks; fully independent at 8 weeks

edators: fisher, fox, bobcat, owl and coyote

Tracks: show 4 or 5 pointed toes around a C-shaped heel pad; often seen along water's edge

scription: The mink has glossy rich brown or black , with a white chin patch and occasional white spots the belly. It has small rounded ears.

1¾"

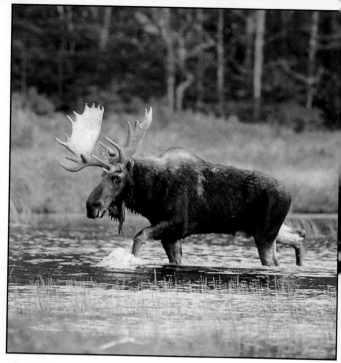

DID YOU KNOW...? A moose can store over 100 lbs. of food in its stomach. It has weak eyesight and has been known to mistake cars for potential mates. The moose will stand and face any adversary. It can run 35 mph and can easily swim 10 miles.

crepuscular

Moose

Alces alces

Size: body 7½-10' long; tail 7"; stands 5-6½' at shoulder; weighs 800-1,800 lbs.

Habitat: forests, regenerating clearcuts, wet woodlands and swamps

Range: northeast, central and western Massachusetts

Food: aspen, maple and cherry trees and water lilies

Mating: September to November; gestation of 8 months; males attract females by making "wallows," which are patches of muddy ground where they urinate

Bedding Site: brushy areas of trampled vegetation

Young: 1 or 2 calves born reddish brown; 25-33 lbs. each; nurse for several months; independent at 1 year

edators: none in Massachusetts

Tracks: heart-shaped with split hoof

scription: The world's largest deer, the moose is dark own to black with a shoulder hump and a flap of skin, lled a dewlap or bell, that hangs below the throat. Males ow flattened antlers under a layer of velvet skin that peels is scraped away. The rack can be more than 5' across d is shed each winter.

6½"

DID YOU KNOW...? The muskrat creates a V-shaped wave as it swims. It can hold its breath underwater for up to 15 minutes. This skill is important as the muskrat works with cattails grass and mud to build huts in the water. The huts measure up to 2' high and 3' across and a good hut can be used by several generations.

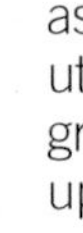

crepuscular nocturnal

MUSKRAT

Ondatra zibethicus

Size: body 9-13" long; tail 7-12" long; weighs 2-4 lbs.

Habitat: marshes, ponds, rivers, streams and lakes with thick vegetation that do not entirely freeze

Range: throughout Massachusetts except Nantucket

Food: pondweeds, cattails, frogs, crayfish and freshwater clams

Mating: mid-March to September; gestation of 25–30 days

Den: may dig a den in stream or river banks or lines a nest chamber with cattails, grass and weeds

Young: 6-8 young per litter; 2-3 litters per year; young born blind; weigh ¾ of an ounce; eyes open at 14-18 days; nurse for 3-4 weeks; independent at 4 weeks

edators: Red-tailed Hawk, mink, Great Horned Owl, Bald Eagle, fox, coyote and raccoon

Tracks: although they have 5 toes on each foot, only 4 show clear imprint; hind feet partly webbed

scription: The muskrat is a light brown to black rodent h slightly lighter undersides and a long, rat-like, nearly irless tail. In winter, muskrats gnaw a hole in the ice and sh vegetation up through it. These are called pushups d are used as feeding sites.

1¼"

2"

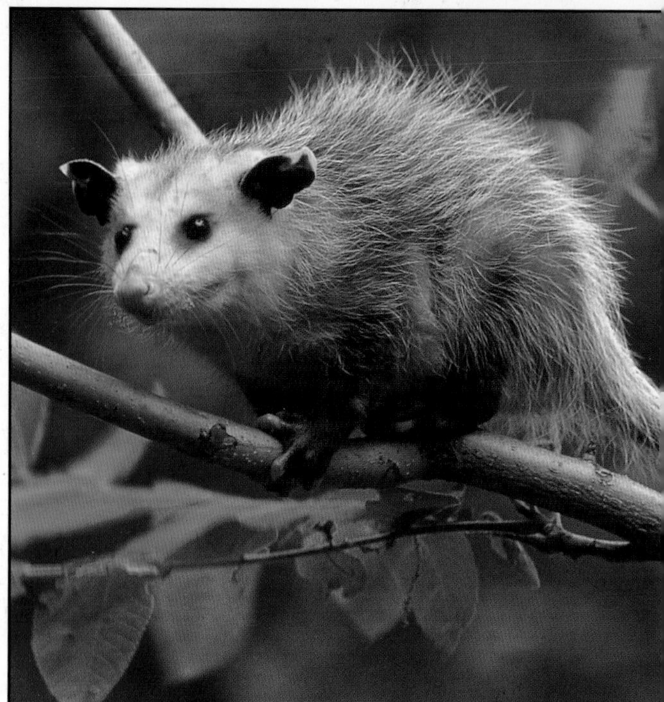

DID YOU KNOW...? When cornered, an opossum will fall into a death-like state, (therefore the term playing possum) for up to 3 hours. It is the only marsupial (pouched) animal native to North America, and it has 50 teeth, more than any other land mammal on this continent. The opossum is an agile climber and good swimmer. It has a prehensile (grasping) tail that it can use to stabilize itself as it walks along tree branches. In winter, it rests in abandoned burrows and hollow trees.

nocturnal

Opossum, Virginia

Didelphis virginiana

Size: body 18-21" long; tail 9-14" long; weighs about 10 lbs.

Habitat: woodlands and brushy areas; suburban areas

Range: throughout Massachusetts except Dukes and Nantucket Counties

Food: eggs, grain, fruit and garbage

Mating: January to early July; gestation of 2 weeks

Den Site: none; immediately after birth, young crawl into mother's kangaroo-like pouch and each attaches to one of 13 nipples

Young: 6-13 kits per litter; 1-2 litters per year; kits are born blind and hairless without well-developed rear limbs; ½" long; less than 1 oz. each; nurse inside the pouch for 8 weeks, then ride on the mother's back for 4 weeks and fully independent at 12 weeks

'redators: dog, bobcat, coyote, fox, hawk and owl

Tracks: hand-like tracks show thumb on hind foot; tail drags between feet

escription: The opossum is grayish white with hairless ırs and tail, and a white face with a long, pink-nosed ıout.

1¾"

DID YOU KNOW...? The otter's torpedo-shaped body allows it to glide effortlessly through the water. An otter can tread water and swim on its front, back and sides. The otter uses slides or shoreline chutes into the water, and otter rolls, which are bowl-shaped areas 20-100' from the water where it dries off and marks territory.

nocturnal *crepuscular*

Otter, River

Lontra canadensis

Size: body 18-32" long; tail 11-20" long; weighs 10-30 lbs.

Habitat: lakes, rivers and streams; favors beaver ponds

Range: throughout Massachusetts except Nantucket and perhaps Suffolk Counties

Food: fish, minnows, frogs, mussels, salamanders, snakes, crayfish and turtles

Mating: March to April; gestation of 60-63 days (after a delayed period of 9-10 months after mating)

Den: located near water and lined with plant material; may use upturned logs, upturned stumps, muskrat or beaver lodges

Young: 1-5 pups born blind and fur covered; 5 oz. each; eyes open at 1 month; young explore outside the den at 2 months; continue to nurse for 4 months; fully independent at 6 months

edators: bobcat, domestic dog and coyote

Tracks: often hidden by dragging tail; front and hind feet show 5 toes

scription: The otter is long and sleek with a muscular and dark brown coat. It has a layer of fat, dense fur, bbed feet, a long tapered tail and valves that keep ter out of its ears and nose.

3"

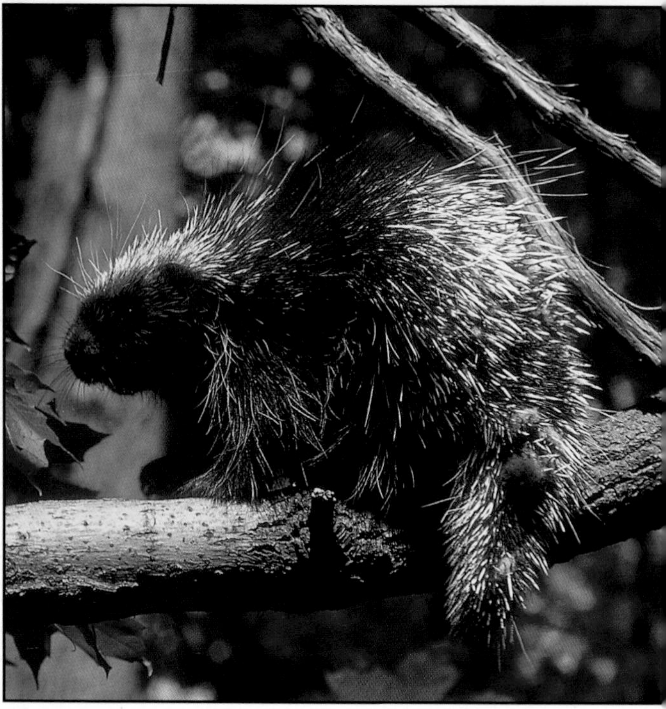

DID YOU KNOW...? Approximately 30,000 quills provide the porcupine with a unique defense. When confronted by a would-be attacker, it swats the animal (or person) with its tail, which is loaded with needle-sharp 4" quills. It does not shoot its quills. Barbed ends cause the quills to work their way deeper into the attacker's muscles, making them difficult to extract.

nocturnal

PORCUPINE

Erethizon dorsatum

Size: body 18-23" long; tail 6-12" long; 10-28 lbs.

Habitat: mixed forests with rock ledges

Range: northeast, central and western Massachusetts

Food: bark, buds and needles of pine and hemlock; leaves, grass, flowers, fruit and seeds

Mating: October to December; gestation of 200-217 days

Den: rock ledges, hollow logs, tree cavities, under stumps and buildings, and in the abandoned burrows of other animals

Young: a single pup born with dark fur and soft 1" quills; 1 lb.; pup nurses for 3 months; fully independent at 5 months

edators: bobcat, coyote and fisher

Tracks: show long nails and bumpy pads; often hidden by dragging tail

escription: The porcupine is a large, round-bodied dent. It has color variations that include dark gray, dark own and black, with thousands of sharp quills. They end the day resting in trees.

2⅝"

3⅜"

DID YOU KNOW...? The raccoon is an excellent climber and swimmer. Contrary to popular belief, it does not wash everything it eats. Clever and agile, the raccoon is highly adapted to gathering and eating a great variety of foods. In the fall, it develops a thick layer of fat.

Raccoon

Procyon lotor

Size: body 16-28" long; tail 8-12" long; stands 12" high at the shoulder; weighs 15-40 lbs.

Habitat: woodlands near open fields, rivers and ponds, suburban and urban areas

Range: throughout Massachusetts except Nantucket

Food: berries, insects, crayfish, garden vegetables, grain, rodents, turtle and bird eggs, carrion (remains of dead animals) and garbage

Mating: January to mid-March; gestation of 63 days

Den: in hollow trees, woodchuck burrows, under buildings, in attics and chimneys

Young: 2-7 young born blind, with a light fur covering, a faint mask, and ringed tail; 4" long; 2 oz. each; eyes open at 21 days; nurse for several weeks; leave den at 10 weeks; independent at 4-6 months

'edators: coyote, fox and bobcat

Tracks: small, hand-like prints

escription: The raccoon has heavy fur streaked brown, ack and gray with a distinctive black face mask and a ishy, ringed tail. It is commonly seen raiding garbage ns. It often spends daytime resting in trees.

3"

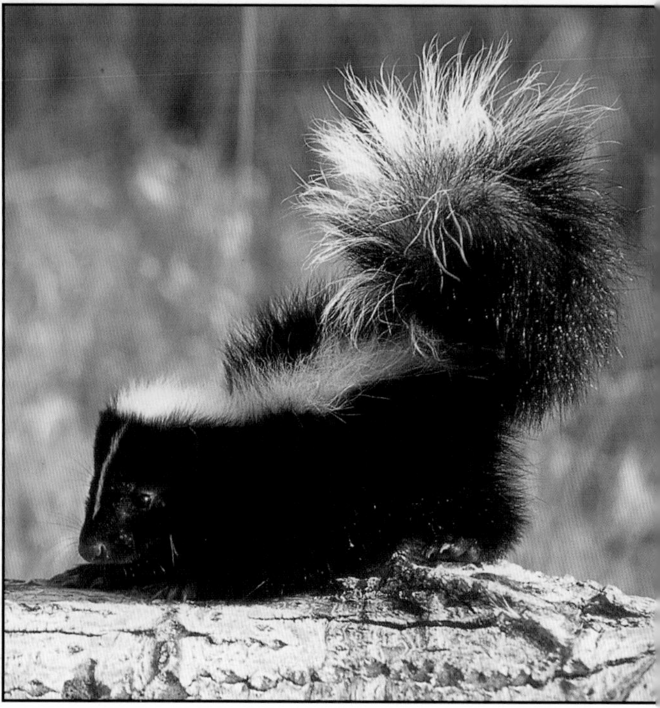

DID YOU KNOW...? The skunk is famous for defending itself from predators up to 20' away with a foul-smelling spray. Even a 3-week-old kit can spray! Before spraying, a skunk usually hisses, stomps its front feet and waves its tail in warning.

Skunk, Striped

Mephitis mephitis

Size: body 15" long; tail 7-8"; weighs 3-10 lbs.

Habitat: forest edges with open areas; prefers to be near water; suburban areas

Range: throughout Massachusetts except Nantucket

Food: insects, small mammals, eggs, fruit, vegetation, garbage and carrion (remains of dead animals)

Mating: February to March; gestation of 62-66 days

Den: under wood piles and buildings, in abandoned burrows, stone walls and in culverts

Young: 5-7 kits born blind, with a distinct black and white pattern; 7 oz.; eyes open at 3 weeks; one litter per year; weaned at 8 weeks and independent at 10 weeks

edators: Great Horned Owl; bobcat and coyote on occasion

Tracks: show five toes and claw marks across each foot

escription: The striped skunk has a glossy black coat th a thin white stripe between the eyes and a broad white shaped stripe on its back and down its bushy tail.The ount of white varies among skunks.

1"

DID YOU KNOW...? An Eastern gray squirrel can hide 25 nuts in half an hour. It usually finds four out of five of the nuts it buries. Nuts are also stored in tree cavities. The squirrel later finds hidden nuts by smell and it can smell a nut buried beneath 12" of snow. Its large bushy tail helps it to maintain balance while jumping from branch to branch.

diurnal

Squirrel, Eastern Gray

Sciurus carolinensis

Size: body 8-11" long; tail 8-11" long; weighs 1½ lbs.

Habitat: wooded areas including forests, parks and backyards

Range: throughout Massachusetts

Food: nuts, seeds (including pinecones), fruits, insects, bird eggs, buds and tree bark; stores surplus food 3-4" underground

Mating: twice a year during January to February and May to June; gestation of 45 days

Den Site: a late winter or spring litter is often born in a tree hollow; a summer litter is born in a 12-19" ball-shaped treetop nest made of leaves, twigs and bark

Young: 2-3 young born blind and hairless; weigh ½ an ounce; eyes open at 4-5 weeks; nurse for 8 weeks; independent at 12 weeks

Predators: bear, bobcat, coyote, fisher, hawk and Great Horned Owl

Tracks: front print shows 4 toes, hind shows 5 toes and is about 1" wide and 2½" long

Description: The Eastern gray squirrel is mostly gray with white underside and a big bushy tail. Melanistic (black) individuals can be found throughout Massachusetts.

2½"

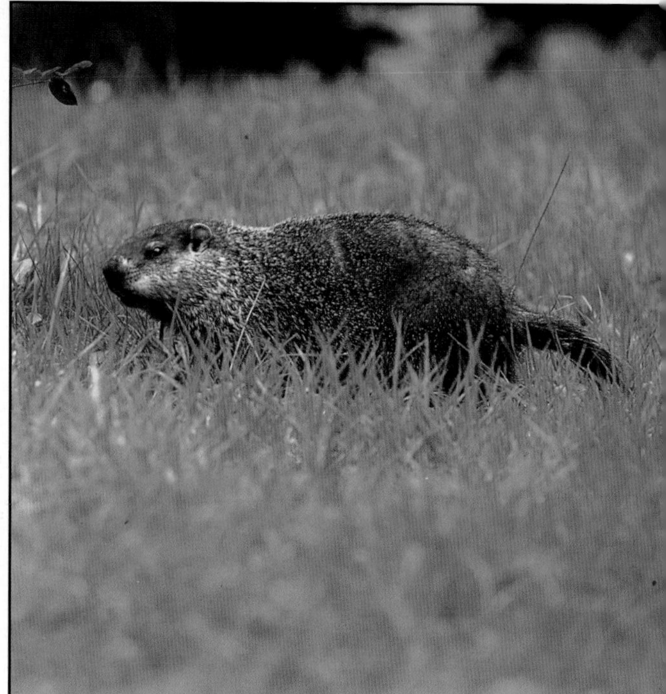

DID YOU KNOW...? A woodchuck can dig a tunnel 5' long in one day. Their burrows often contain a network of tunnels up to 40' long. An active burrow usually has fresh dirt in front of it and has many entrances. Woodchucks begin hibernating as early as September and remain in the burrow for up to six months. The woodchuck is also known as the groundhog, but despite having Groundhog's Day named for it, it can't really predict when winter will end.

diurnal Zzz *hibernator*

Woodchuck

Marmota monax

Size: body 12-23" long; tail 4-10" long; weighs 4-14 lbs.

Habitat: open woodlands, farmland, pastures, fields and grassy areas

Range: throughout Massachusetts except Dukes and Nantucket Counties

Food: dandelions, grass, garden vegetables, clover, bark and twigs

Mating: early March to April; gestation of 28-30 days

Den: grass-lined burrows, located 4½' underground

Young: 2-6 young born blind and hairless; 4" long and weigh 1 ounce; young nurse for 4 weeks and are fully independent at 3 months

redators: domestic dog, fox, hawk, bobcat and coyote

Tracks: front print shows 4 toes, hind print shows 5; rarely seen

escription: The woodchuck is a large ground mammal
th coarse yellow brown to black fur, short legs and ears
d a blunt nose. It's found in areas with soft, well-drained
il, near good vegetation and water. Woodchucks spend
ne sunning near a burrow entrance.

2"

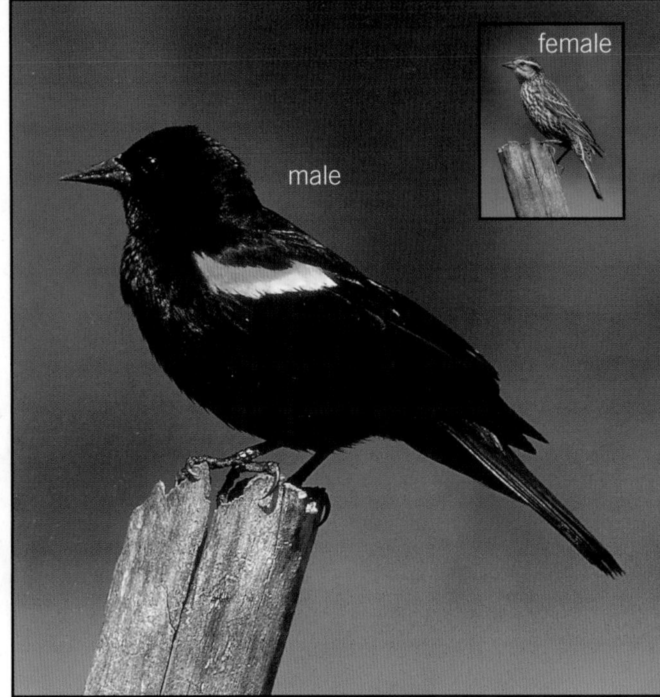

DID YOU KNOW...? Male and female Red-winged Blackbirds do not migrate together. The males return to the breeding area several weeks before the females, usually while snow is still on the ground. The male establishes and defends a nesting site to attract one or more females.

Blackbird, Red-winged

Agelaius phoeniceus

Size: body 7½-9½" long; 10-12" wingspan; 1.6 oz.

Habitat: wetlands near trees and open areas

Range: throughout Massachusetts

Food: seeds and insects

Nesting: May to June

Nest: bowl-shaped cup of grass, reeds and roots attached to marsh vegetation 3-14" above water; cattails provide protection from weather and predators

Eggs: average clutch 3-5; pale blue marked with purple and black spots and streaks; 2-3 broods per year

Young: hatch in 11 days; females tend the eggs; males defend the nest; young hatch blind and featherless; eyes open at 1 week; flight feathers develop at 10 days; young leave nesting area at 20 days

'redators: Sharp-shinned Hawk, Cooper's Hawk and Great Horned Owl

ligration: present in summer; migrates to southern states

escription: Males are black with a bright red and gold ing patch and the females are streaked brown-and-white. uring migration, they often flock with other species of ackbirds, such as grackles and cowbirds.

DID YOU KNOW...? The Eastern Bluebird has tremendous eyesight. It is capable of seeing an insect 100 feet away. In the fall, it may form large roosting flocks of up to 50 birds that huddle together at night to conserve heat. The bluebird will generally return to the same nesting site year after year if it is properly maintained. Populations have declined due to the introduction of House Sparrows and European Starlings, which compete with bluebirds for nest sites. Nest box programs have helped to enhance bluebird populations.

Bluebird, Eastern

Sialia sialis

Size: body 7" long; 13" wingspan; 1.1 oz.

Habitat: fields, meadows and orchards

Range: throughout Massachusetts

Food: insects, seeds and berries

Nesting: April to July

Nest: tree cavities such as woodpecker holes and nest boxes 5-12' above ground; 4-5 day nest construction primarily built by the female; the nest is lined with feathers or fine grasses

Eggs: average clutch of 4-5; pale blue; 2-3 broods per year

Young: hatch in 13-15 days; blind and featherless; eyes open at 1 week; fully feathered within 2 weeks; male and female care for the young for up to 6 weeks; leaves the nest at 3 weeks

edators: small mammals, snake and other birds including House Sparrow, European Starling and House Wren that kill the young

igration: present in summer; most migrate to southern states, but some remain in Massachusetts for the winter

scription: The male is bright blue with a rust-col-
d breast and white undersides; the female is grayish
e with a rust-colored breast and white undersides

DID YOU KNOW...? The Northern Cardinal is very territoria
It has been known to attack its reflection in windows. It
named after the red-robed Cardinals of the Roman Cathol
Church. Seven states have identified the cardinal as their sta
bird, more than any other bird.

Cardinal, Northern

Cardinalis cardinalis

Size: body 7-9" long; 12" wingspan; 1.6 oz.

Habitat: forest edges, parks, brushy fields and residential areas

Range: throughout Massachusetts

Food: insects, seeds, fruit and berries

Nesting: April to June; during courtship males can be seen feeding females, especially at feeders

Nest: often found in pine trees; constructed of twigs and lined with grass; nest is usually 10' above ground

Eggs: average clutch 3-4; pale blue spotted with brown; 2-3 broods per year

Young: hatch in 12-13 days; young hatch blind and featherless; eyes open at 1 week; flight feathers develop at 10 days; males help care for young; young leave nesting area at 20 days

Predators: Cooper's Hawk, Sharp-shinned Hawk, Great Horned Owl and domestic cat

Migration: present year-round

Description: Male cardinals are bright red with a prominent crest and a black face. The females are brownish yellow with a hint of red; both have a large, reddish orange, cone-shaped bill.

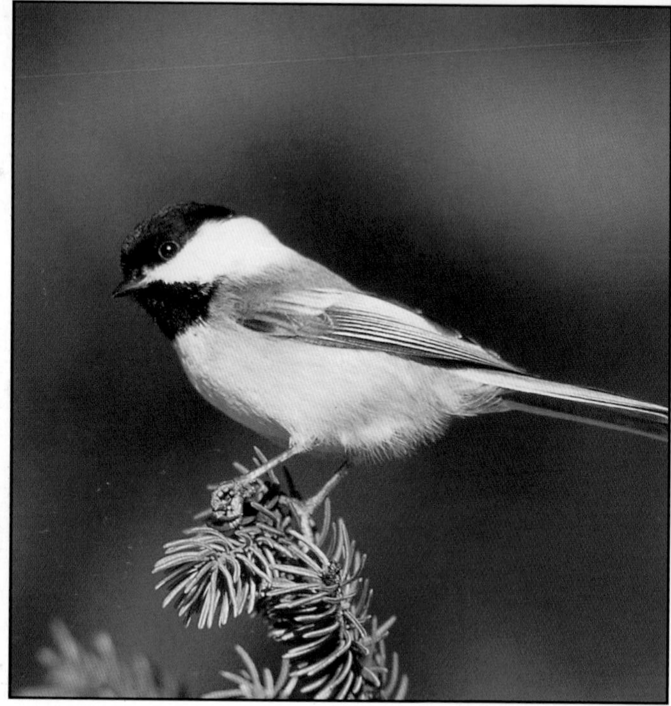

DID YOU KNOW...? Black-capped Chickadees are incredibly acrobatic, hopping along trees as they search for food. They also have the specialized leg muscles that allow them to hang upside-down on a branch while feeding. They can slowly climb up a nearly vertical tree. "Chick-a-dee-dee-dee" is the frequently heard call of the Black-capped Chickadee and the origin of its name. It is the state bird of Massachusetts.

Chickadee, Black-capped

Poecile atricapillus

Size: 5-5½" long; 8" wingspan; weighs ½ oz.

Habitat: mixed forests, parks and residential areas

Range: throughout Massachusetts

Food: insects, seeds and berries

Nesting: May to July; pairs form in early fall and last until early spring

Nest: excavates holes in dead tree; also uses bird houses and existing cavities from other birds such as woodpeckers; fur or feather lined; usually 4-10' above ground

Eggs: average clutch 6-8; creamy white with red or purple speckles; 1-2 broods per year

Young: hatch blind and featherless in 11-13 days; eyes open at 1 week; flight feathers appear at 10-14 days; female tends to young although male brings food to female; fly at 14-18 days

redators: Northern Shrike, Eastern Screech-Owl and Sharp-shinned Hawk

ligration: present year-round

escription: The Black-capped Chickadee has a short, ump body, with a black cap and throat, white cheeks and elly, and a gray back and tail. The male is slightly larger an the female.

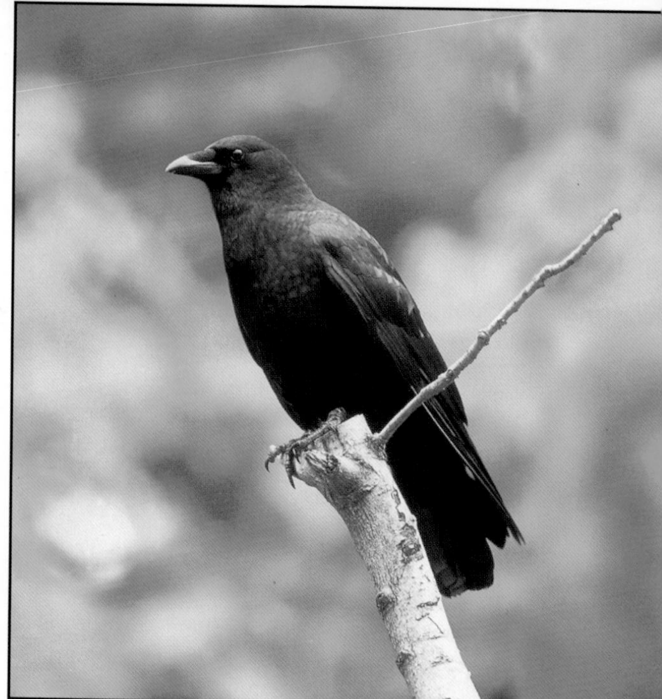

DID YOU KNOW...? The loud and familiar caw-caw of the American Crow is common throughout the state. It usually forms small, noisy flocks of 4-7 birds; during the fall and winter months it roosts in massive flocks that number in the hundreds to thousands. It can often be seen along roadsides feeding on carrion. The American Crow is considered to be an intelligent bird capable of imitating many sounds.

Crow, American

Corvus brachyrhynchos

Size: 17-21" long; 18" wingspan; 3-6 oz.

Habitat: fields and wooded areas

Range: throughout Massachusetts

Food: fruit, insects, worms, fish, seeds, small mammals, eggs, nuts and carrion (remains of dead animals); regurgitates oval pellets of indigestible bone, feathers and hair

Nesting: March to June

Nest: bulky; constructed of sticks; adults may return to the same nesting site each year; nest is usually 10-70' above ground in the crotch of a tree

Eggs: average clutch size 3-8; greenish blue with brown splotches; 1 brood per year

Young: hatch blind and featherless in 18 days; eyes open at 1 week; feathers develop within 10 days; young leave the nest at 28-35 days

redators: hawk, falcon and owl

ligration: present year-round

scription: The American Crow, usually referred to as e Common Crow, is fairly large in size. It is black all over th broad wings and a squared tail.

DID YOU KNOW...? The Mourning Dove is named for its sad-sounding coo. The crop milk (partially digested food that is regurgitated) it provides its young is more nutritious than cow's milk. It is the most abundant and widespread dove in the U.S. It is able to reach flight speeds of 60 mph.

Dove, Mourning

Zenaida macroura

Size: 10-12" long; 18" wingspan; 3-6 oz.

Habitat: open wooded areas, orchards and residential areas

Range: throughout Massachusetts

Food: seeds and grains

Nesting: April to July

Nest: loosely constructed of twigs; found in pine trees or shrubs 10-25' off the ground, or on the ground

Eggs: average clutch of 2; white, unmarked eggs; 2-3 broods per year

Young: hatch in 13-14 days; young hatch blind and featherless; eyes open at 1 week; feathers develop within 10 days; the male and female provide the young with crop milk (partially digested food that is regurgitated); young leave the nest at 12-14 days

redators: hawk, owl, cat, Blue Jay and squirrel

Iigration: present year-round

escription: The Mourning Dove is grayish brown with ht, pinkish brown head, chest and undersides. It has a ht blue ring around its eye, a black bill, red legs and a ng pointed tail edged with white.

DID YOU KNOW...? The Rock Dove, more commonly referred to as Pigeon or Feral Pigeon, originally came to the U.S. from Europe and Asia. It has a unique homing ability and has been used to carry messages for many years, especially during wartime. It is unknown how Rock Doves are able to navigate but some scientists speculate that the birds use landmarks and/or Earth's magnetic field. An agile flyer, it can reach speeds of 80 mph.

Dove, Rock

Columba livia

Size: 11-14" long; wingspan 28"; 9 oz.

Habitat: open wooded areas, cliffs, urban parks and bridges

Range: throughout Massachusetts

Food: seeds and buds

Nesting: occurs year-round

Nest: commonly located with other nests under a bridge or on the side of a building

Eggs: average clutch size is 2; white eggs; 2-3 broods each year

Young: hatch in 18 days; young hatch blind and featherless; eyes open at 1 week; feathers develop within 2 weeks; the male and female provide the young with crop milk (partially digested food that is regurgitated); young leave the nesting area at 35 days

edators: hawk, falcon and crow

igration: present year-round

scription: The Rock Dove color varies greatly including ıe-gray, black, rust and white. It often has an iridescent-rple neck, barred wings, a black-banded tail and white mp. It has short red legs.

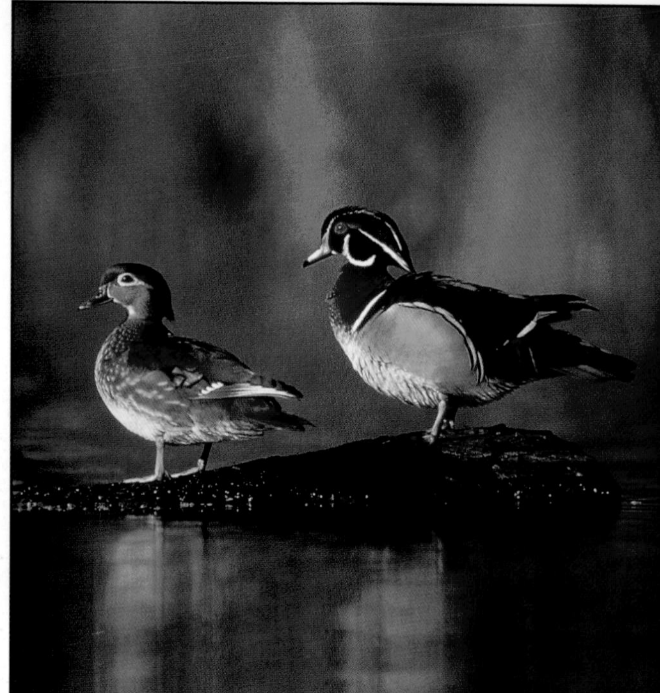

DID YOU KNOW...? The Wood Duck is commonly callec Woodie. Population numbers declined drastically in the early 1900s due to wetland drainage, unregulated hunting and logging. An experimental nesting box project was initiated in ar attempt to boost the Wood Duck population. Today, nes boxes hang in and around lakes, ponds and streams across the country and Wood Duck populations are very strong Wood Ducks have broad wings that make a distinct flapping sound as they fly.

Duck, Wood

Aix sponsa

Size: body 18½" long; 30" wingspan; 1½ lbs.

Habitat: wooded areas near water

Range: throughout Massachusetts

Food: insects, acorns, hickory nuts, seeds of aquatic plants, grains and fruit

Nesting: March to July

Nest: abandoned woodpecker holes or artificial nesting boxes 20-50' above ground; lined with down; adults often return to same nesting site each year

Eggs: average clutch 8-15; white; 1 brood each year; egg-dumping is common (egg dumping means a female lays one or more eggs in another nest where they are cared for)

Young: hatch in 27-30 days; jump from the nest within 24 hours of hatching; can feed themselves immediately; able to fly at 8-9 weeks

redators: raccoon preys on eggs; snake, fish, hawk, snapping turtle, muskrat and otter prey on young

ligration: migrates in early fall to southern states

escription: The male Wood Duck has red eyes and a stinct crest on its head and is brilliantly colored with iriscent shades of chestnut, purple and green. Female grayish brown, which camouflages her from predators.

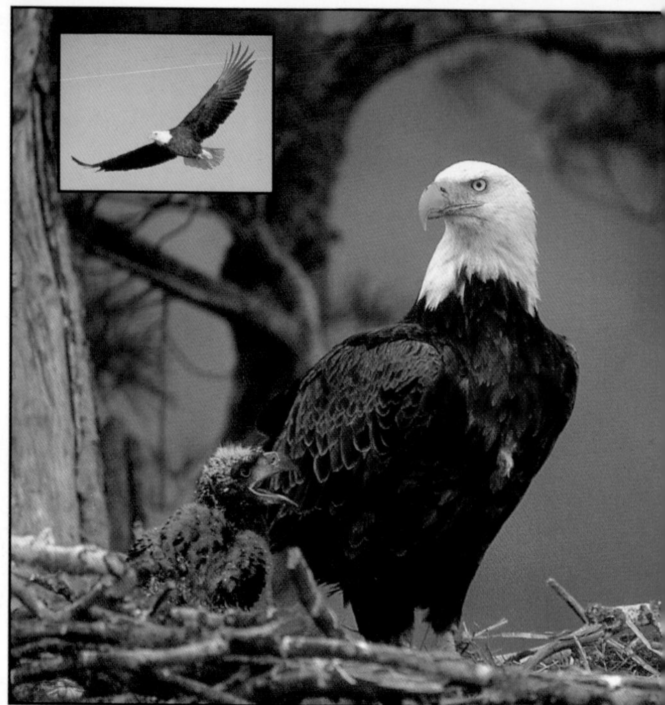

DID YOU KNOW...? Unique to North America, the Bald Eagle was chosen as our nation's symbol in 1782, narrowly beating out the Wild Turkey. A powerful bird of prey, the Bald Eagle catches its prey with its razor-sharp talons by swooping down at speeds of 50 mph. It was placed on the Federal Endangered Species list in 1972 due to agricultural pesticide contamination. Since the pesticide DDT was banned, the Bald Eagle population has recovered.

Eagle, Bald

Haliaeetus leucocephalus

Size: body 3-3½' long; 6½-8' wingspan; 8-14 lbs.

Habitat: forested areas near rivers and lakes

Range: throughout Massachusetts

Food: fish make up 90% of diet; waterfowl, gulls, turtles and carrion; regurgitates pellets of indigestible parts of prey

Nesting: March to May; mated pairs return to the same nest site each spring

Nest: located in tall, live trees 50-60' above ground

Eggs: average clutch 1-3; large, dull-white; 1 brood per year; male and female care for eggs

Young: eaglets hatch in 35 days covered with gray down; 4 oz. each; male and female care for young; by 10-12 weeks grow brown feathers flecked with white; develop adult coloration, including white head, at 4-5 years

redators: raccoons prey on eggs and nestlings

ligration: present year-round; population increases in winter due to migrants from farther north

escription: The Bald Eagle is a large, dark brown bird th a white head and tail. Its eyes and beak are bright yel- w. Each winter over 60 eagles gather at Quabbin eservoir and along the Connecticut River where sev- al pairs remain to nest.

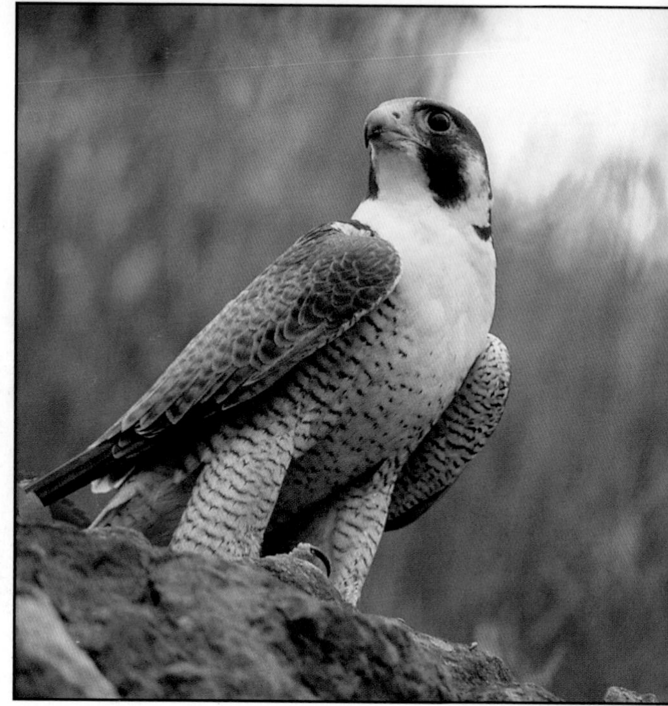

DID YOU KNOW...? A strong bird of prey, the Peregrine Falcon swoops down on its prey at speeds of more than 185 mph. Peregrine comes from the word *peregrinate* which means to travel or wander. This falcon was placed on the Federal Endangered Species list in 1984 due to agricultural pesticide contamination and removed from the list in 1999. Banning the pesticide DDT has helped, and captive breeding programs have been successful.

Falcon, Peregrine

Falco peregrinus

Size: body 16-20" long; 40-45" wingspan; 19-40 oz.

Habitat: skyscrapers, bridges and cliffs

Range: throughout Massachusetts

Food: birds comprise most of the falcon's diet; it regurgitates pellets containing the indigestible parts of their prey, including bones, feathers and hair

Nesting: March to May

Nest: no real nest constructed; lays eggs on loose gravel on cliffs, bridges and skyscrapers

Eggs: average clutch 2-5; creamy white speckled with brown; 1 brood per year

Young: hatch in 28-29 days; young covered with white down; male and female care for young, feeding them mice and birds; young develop feathers at 3 weeks and leave the nest at 6-9 weeks

redators: Great Horned Owl

ligration: most migrate to southern states, but some remain in Massachusetts for the winter

escription: Usually found near water, the Peregrine is ownish gray to slate blue with a dark face mask and hter undersides that are streaked with black or brown.

no nest

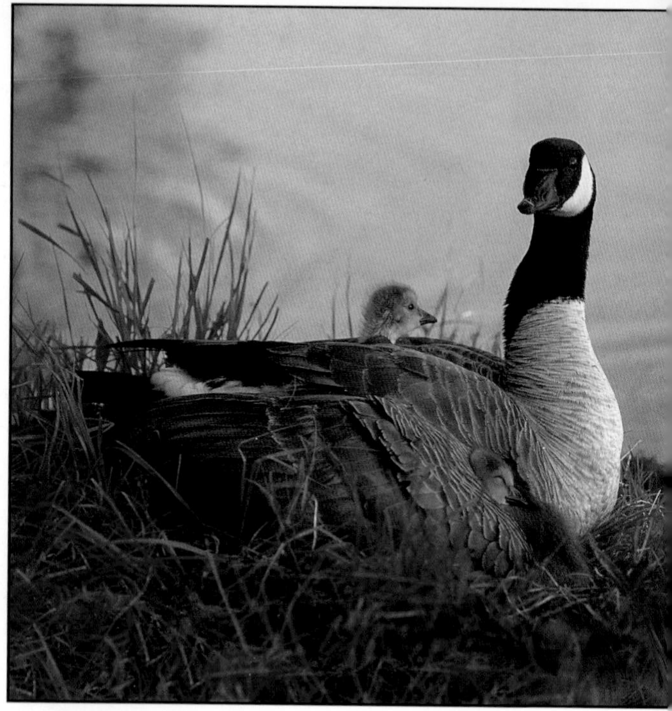

DID YOU KNOW...? The Canada Goose is nicknamed honker, because of the distinct honking sound it makes. Not all honkers migrate, but some travel from winter resting and feeding grounds in the south to summer nesting grounds in the north. They migrate in V-shaped flocks, sometimes flying as far as 4,000 miles.

Goose, Canada

Branta canadensis

Size: body 22-40" long; 5-6' wingspan; 2-18 lbs.

Habitat: grassy fields, lakes, ponds, marshes and rivers

Range: throughout Massachusetts

Food: aquatic plants, insects, grass seeds, crops

Nesting: April to June; pairs mate for life

Nest: grass lined depression on a raised site near water's edge

Eggs: average clutch 5; large and creamy white

Young: hatch in 25-30 days; young are covered with yellowish down; males and females tend young; leave the nest at 45 days

Predators: larger meat-eating mammals, Great Horned Owl; goslings may be taken by snapping turtle

Migration: some migrate to southern states, but most remain in Massachusetts for the winter

escription: Found in rural, suburban and urban areas, he Canada Goose is a large, light gray goose with a white hinstrap. It has a black head, neck, bill and feet. Its tracks re triangular and webbed and it moves between wetlands nd farmlands or open grasslands. It is most active during he morning and afternoon.

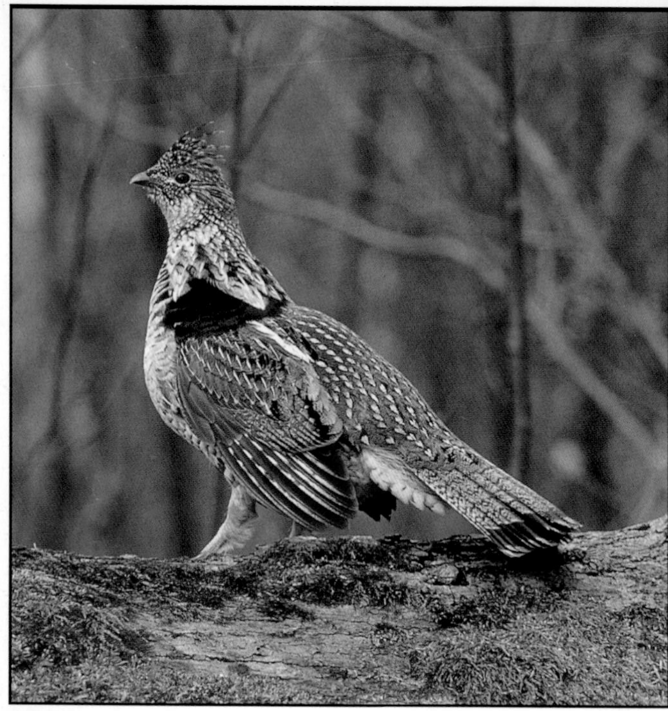

Did You Know...? The Ruffed Grouse gets its name from the ruff of dark feathers on each side of its neck. Its wings are short and wide for rapid bursts of flight and can reach speeds of 40 mph. It has special comb-like membranes on its feet, allowing it to walk easily across the snow. On bitter cold days, it may burrow into the snow, which provides insulated shelter like an igloo.

Grouse, Ruffed

Bonasa umbellus

Size: body 16-19" long; 22-25" wingspan; 1½ lbs.

Habitat: dense woodlands with open areas

Range: throughout Massachusetts except Nantucket and Suffolk Counties

Food: seeds, insects, fruits and leaves

Nesting: April to June; males stand on a log or stone wall and drum the air by flapping their wings vigorously, creating a "thump, thump, thump" sound that can be heard up to a half mile away

Nest: hens build nest on ground, often at base of trees

Eggs: average clutch 9-12; creamy white; 1 brood per year

Young: hatch in 24 days; precocial (covered with feathers and able to feed themselves); young can fly short distances at 12 days; they stay with female for 3-4 months

redators: fox, coyote, Cooper's Hawk, Northern Goshawk and Great Horned Owl

ligration: present year-round

escription: The Grouse is a gray chicken-like bird with cks of black, white and brown and has a square, fan-aped tail. It also has crown-like tufts of feathers on its ad.

DID YOU KNOW...? The Herring Gull has long, slender wings that allow it to glide effortlessly at speeds of 25 mph. It has an elongated, hooked bill that makes catching small fish (especially herring) easy. A voracious scavenger, the Herring Gull forms noisy flocks that congregate around fishing boats, picnic grounds and landfills. It seldom travels more than 2 miles from land.

GULL, HERRING

Larus argentatus

Size: 22" long; 55" wingspan; 2½ lbs.

Habitat: shorelines, beaches, lakes, rivers and landfills

Range: throughout Massachusetts

Food: fish, crabs, clams, insects, birds and garbage

Nesting: May to August

Nest: nesting colonies on the coast; ground nester; loosely constructed of sticks, rocks and seaweed

Eggs: average clutch 2-5; olive-buff with dark brown speckles; 1 brood per year

Young: hatch in 24-28 days; eyes are open; mobile; adults feed the young regurgitated food; leave the nest at 35 days

edators: fox, weasel, domestic cat and Great Horned Owl

igration: present year-round; birds move around Massachusetts in winter to be near large bodies of open water

scription: Juvenile Herring Gulls are mottled brown or ay with a black bill. The adult is pearly white with gray ngs, back and rump. Its wing tips are black with white ots, and its bill is bright yellow with a red spot. The erring Gull has pinkish legs.

DID YOU KNOW...? The Red-tail is a powerful raptor (bird o prey). It has eyesight many times greater than humans anc can see a small mouse or rat from hundreds of feet in the air Listen for its high-pitched screams as it circles above its prey then dives down to snatch it with its sharp talons. The hawk has a sharp, curved beak adapted for tearing its prey intc pieces as it eats.

Hawk, Red-tailed

Buteo jamaicensis

Size: body 19-26" long; 4-4½' wingspan; males 1½-2 lbs.; females 2-4 lbs.

Habitat: wetlands, woodlands, fields and along highways

Range: throughout Massachusetts

Food: mice, rabbits, squirrels, snakes, birds and insects; regurgitates pellets of indigestible parts of prey

Nesting: March to April

Nest: 28-38" across; located in tall trees; lined with shredded bark and pine needles; returns to same nest site each year

Eggs: average clutch 4; bluish and speckled; 1 brood per year

Young: hatch in 28-32 days; young are covered with white down; males and females tend young; young leave the nest at 6-7 weeks

redators: none; harassed by crows

ligration: some migrate to southern states, but most remain in Massachusetts for the winter

escription: The Red-tailed Hawk varies in color from uff to brown to black-and-white, with a patterned, reaked underside. It usually has a bright reddish tail nd is often seen perched on telephone poles.

DID YOU KNOW...? The Great Blue Heron is the largest and most common heron species. Often miscalled a crane, Great Blue Herons are often spotted hunting along the water's edge. Their large 4-toed feet help distribute the heron's weight in the same manner as snowshoes, preventing it from sinking into the mud.

Heron, Great Blue

Ardea herodias

Size: body 39-52" long; 6-7' wingspan; 6-12 lbs.

Habitat: shallow lakes, ponds, rivers and wetlands, especially those with standing dead timber

Range: throughout Massachusetts

Food: insects, fish, amphibians and reptiles

Nesting: April to May

Nest: 2-3' across; grouped in large rookeries (colonies) in tall trees along water's edge, nests are built of sticks and often are located over 100' above the ground; nests are used year after year

Eggs: average clutch 3-7; pale blue-green eggs; 1 brood per year

Young: hatch featherless in 26-29 days; male and female care for young by regurgitating food into their mouths; young leave nest at 7-8 weeks

edators: none in Massachusetts

ligration: most migrate to southern states, Central and South America; a few individuals remain in Massachusetts for the winter near open water

escription: The Great Blue Heron has a blue-gray ck with lighter undersides. It has a white head with a ack crest, long neck, long stick-like dark legs, and a ng dagger-like pale yellow bill.

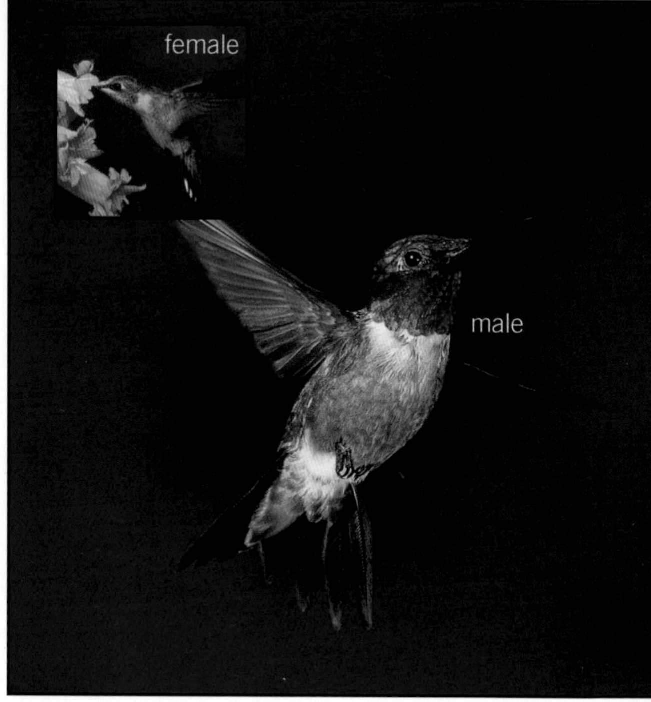

DID YOU KNOW...? The Ruby-throated Hummingbird flies a speeds of more than 60 mph. It can even fly backwards. Its name comes from the humming sound created by the rapic beating of its tiny wings that move at 50 –75 beats per second It migrates to Central America each winter, flying up to 50(miles without resting.

Hummingbird, Ruby-throated

Archilochus colubris

Size: body 3¾" long; 4½" wingspan; 1/10 oz. (about weight of a penny)

Habitat: open woodlands and residential areas

Range: throughout Massachusetts

Food: flower nectar, tree sap, insects and spiders

Nesting: May to July

Nest: cup-shaped; about the size of a walnut shell; built from plant material and spider silk; located 10-20' above ground

Eggs: average clutch 2; white; pea-sized; 1 brood per year

Young: hatch in 16 days; feathers develop at 3-4 days; young leave the nest at 30-34 days

redators: Blue Jay and crow prey on eggs; Cooper's Hawk and Sharp-shinned Hawk

Migration: migrates to southern states and Central America

escription: Hummingbirds are tiny emerald green birds ith light undersides; males have a bright red throat patch nd females have a white throat patch. They are tracted to bright flowers and can be seen hovering om flower to flower, lapping nectar.

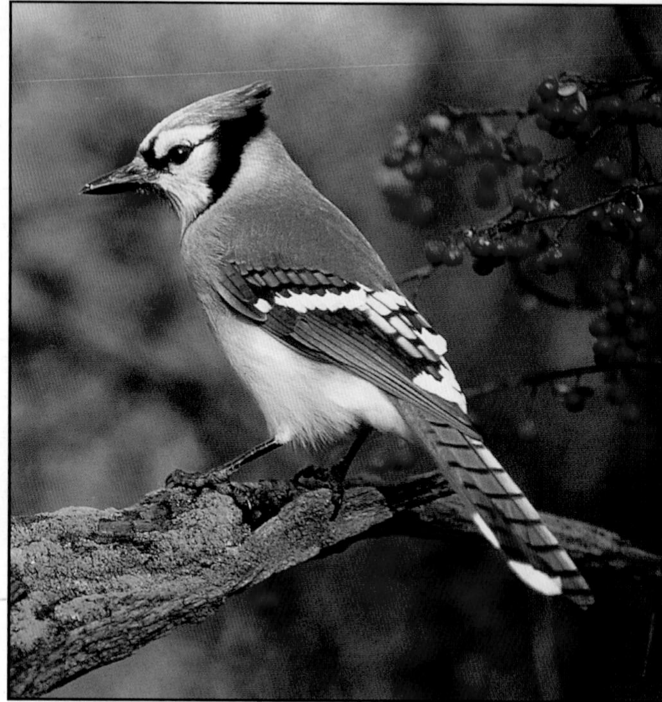

DID YOU KNOW...? A member of the crow family, the Blue Jay is very aggressive. It often scares other birds away from feeders. Its loud cry serves as an alarm for many species of wildlife. A very bold bird, it commonly taunts and mobs birds of prey such as hawks or owls.

Jay, Blue

Cyanocitta cristata

Size: body 11-12" long; 16" wingspan; 3 oz.

Habitat: open wooded areas, parks and backyards

Range: throughout Massachusetts

Food: acorns, insects, fruit, seeds and carrion (remains of dead animals); raids the nests of other birds and eats their eggs and young; stores seeds and acorns that are seldom retrieved

Nesting: April to June

Nest: bulky nests in pine trees, constructed of twigs and lined with grass

Eggs: average clutch 3-6; olive-green spotted with brown; 1-2 broods per year

Young: hatch in 16-18 days; young hatch blind and featherless; eyes open at 1 week; flight feathers develop at 13-20 days; leave nest at 17-23 days

'redators: Cooper's Hawk, Sharp-shinned Hawk, Merlin

ligration: present year-round

escription: The Blue Jay is a bright blue bird with a ack necklace and white barring on its wings. It has a ayish white face and underside with a long wedge-aped tail, and a distinct crest on its head.

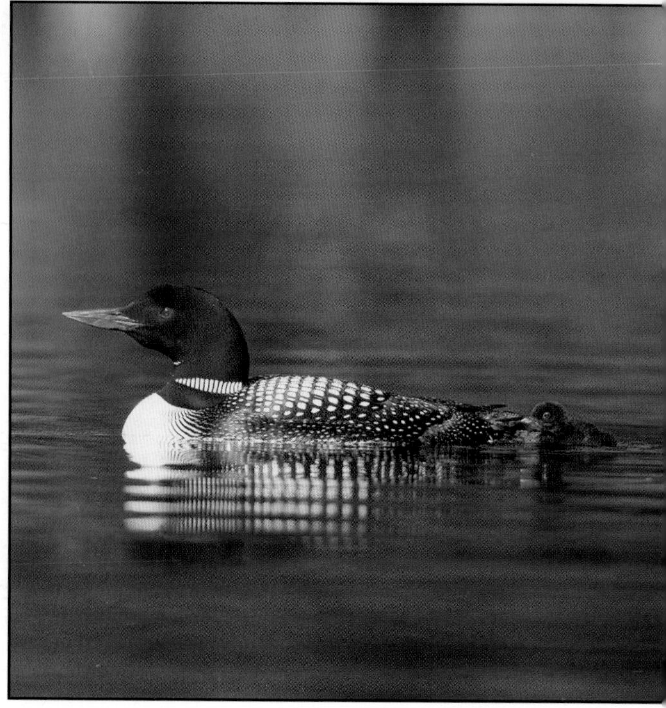

DID YOU KNOW...? The bones of most birds are hollow and lightweight, which aids them in flight. In contrast, the loon has solid bones, which helps it to dive to depths up to 150' in search of food. The adults often carry the young on their backs during the first few weeks. Nesting loons can be found at Quabbin and Wachusett reservoirs.

Loon, Common

Gavia immer

Size: body 28-36" long; 49-58" wingspan; 8-12 lbs.

Habitat: large, deep lakes with islands and bays; reservoirs

Range: throughout Massachusetts

Food: fish, crayfish and insects

Nesting: May to July

Nest: 2' across; commonly found on protected island shoreline on sand or rocks

Eggs: average clutch of 2 olive green eggs speckled with brown; 1 brood per year

Young: hatch in 28 days; young are covered with dark, fuzzy down and are able to leave the nest in 1 day; male and female care for eggs and young; independent at 2-3 months

redators: raccoon preys on eggs; snapping turtle preys on young

ligration: migrates to southern states and Mexico; some remain in Massachusetts for the winter along the coast

escription: The Common Loon has a black and white ıeckered back, a dark greenish black head, a long, ›inted black bill and bright red eyes. It occupies a nge of 10-200 acres and spends most of its time in e water searching for food.

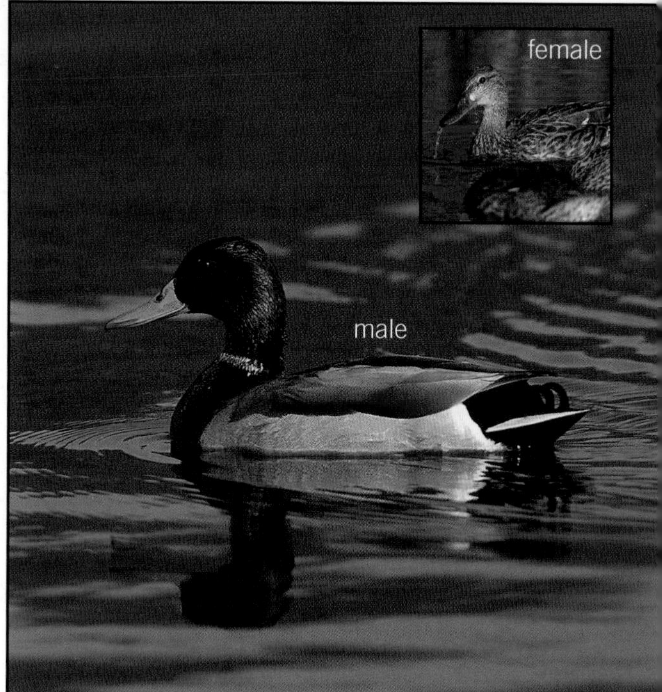

DID YOU KNOW...? Commonly referred to as green head the Mallard is the most abundant and widespread of all water fowl species and can be found almost anywhere in the world It is a dabbling duck (also called puddle duck) and feeds with its tail straight up in the air or by skimming the water jus below the surface. Like all ducks, the Mallard has a lamellate bill, which means it has tooth-like edges that act much like a strainer allowing the duck to hold a piece of food while the water drains through.

Mallard

Anas platyrhynchos

Size: 20-23" long; 36" wingspan; 1-2½ lbs.

Habitat: lakes, ponds, rivers and marshes

Range: throughout Massachusetts

Food: aquatic plants, aquatic insects, grasses, seeds and grains

Nesting: March to July; mating pairs form in fall

Nest: ground nester; bowl-shaped, 7-8" in diameter; lined with vegetation

Eggs: average clutch 8-12; pale green to white; 1 brood per year

Young: hatch in 26-30 days; young are precocial (completely mobile and feed themselves) and leave the nest in 1 day; capable of flight at 60 days

redators: eggs and ducklings fall prey to fox, skunk, coyote, turtle and large fish

ligration: present year-round

escription: The male Mallard is gray with a distinct green ead, thin white collar, rust-colored chest, yellow bill and ange legs. The female is a drab, mottled brown with a dull ange bill.

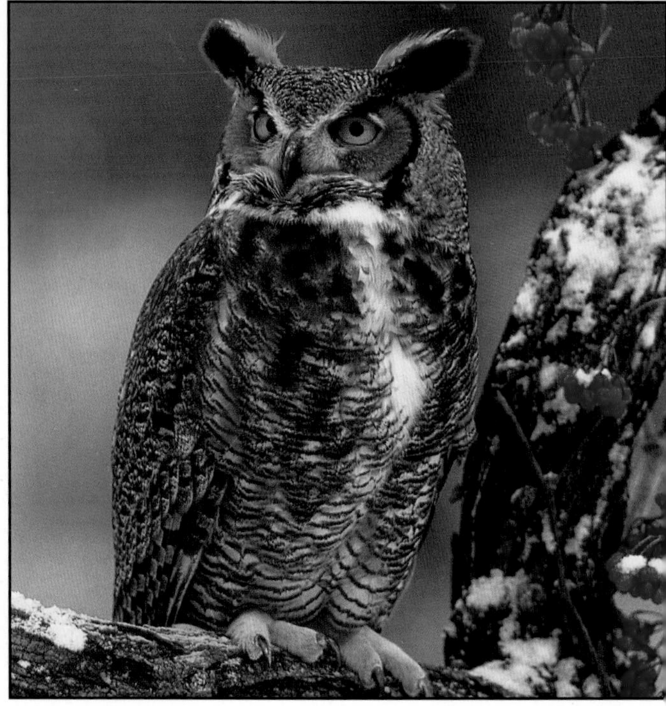

DID YOU KNOW...? A single Great Horned Owl can eat nearly 1,000 mice each year. It has the strongest talons of all owl species. The Great Horned Owl is nicknamed the tiger with wings, because it's one of the few animals that will kill skunks.

Owl, Great Horned

Bubo virginianus

Size: body 18-25" long; 4-5' wingspan; 3-6 lbs.; females slightly larger than males

Habitat: woodlands, forested wetlands and large parks

Range: throughout Massachusetts

Food: rabbits, young skunks, rodents, other small mammals and birds; regurgitates pellets of indigestible parts of prey

Nesting: February to April

Nest: uses tree hollows and abandoned nests of squirrels, hawks, herons and crows

Eggs: average clutch 1-5; white; male brings food to female while she tends the eggs; 1 brood per year

Young: hatch in 28-32 days blind and covered with fine down; eyes open at 7-10 days; young gain flight feathers at 6-9 weeks

edators: none; harassed by crows

igration: present year-round

scription: The Great Horned Owl is a large, reddish own to gray or black owl with lighter, streaked undersides. as a white throat collar, yellow eyes and horn-like tufts of thers on its head. It is most active at night, relying on keen senses of hearing and sight to find its prey.

DID YOU KNOW...? The American Robin uses anting to ri itself of lice and other parasites. The bird positions itself nea an anthill and allows ants to crawl all over its body. Robins ar not listening for worms when they cock their heads from sid to side. Because their eyes are placed far back on the sides c their heads, they must turn their heads from side to side t look at things.

ROBIN, AMERICAN

Turdus migratorius

Size: body 9-11" long; 17" wingspan; 2-3 oz.

Habitat: open woodlands, farmland, orchards and backyards

Range: throughout Massachusetts

Food: earthworms, insects, fruits and berries

Nesting: April to July

Nest: females build nests out of mud, grass and twigs; found in trees, shrubs and house gutters

Eggs: average clutch 3-5; pale blue; 2 broods per year

Young: hatch in 12-14 days; young hatch blind and featherless; eyes open at 1 week; flight feathers develop at 13-20 days

edators: Sharp-shinned Hawk, Cooper's Hawk, raccoon

igration: some migrate to southern states and Central America; others remain in Massachusetts for the winter

scription: Early arrivals each spring, robins are usually ınd poking around lawns in search of earthworms. Males ve slate-gray backs, rusty-red chests and white speck- throats. Females are gray-brown with pale orange ests. They often form large migrating flocks in the fall.

DID YOU KNOW...? The Tree Swallow has an oil glan located at the base of its tail. It uses its beak to smear and coa its feathers with oil each day, which is called preening. Withou proper care, feathers can lose their insulating and waterproof ing capabilities. All birds molt (lose and regrow their feathers once or twice each year. Unlike other swallows, the Tre Swallow does not feed exclusively on insects, which increase it chances of survival as it does not rely solely on one sourc of food.

Swallow, Tree

Tachycineta bicolor

Size: body 5-6" long; 14½" wingspan; 0.7 oz.

Habitat: open areas near water with dead standing trees; often found near beaver ponds

Range: throughout Massachusetts

Food: insects (100 per day), berries and fruit

Nesting: April to June

Nest: cavity nester occupying abandoned woodpecker holes or artificial nesting boxes; lined with grasses and feathers; some form colonies

Eggs: average clutch size 3-8; white; 1 brood per year

Young: hatch blind and featherless in 13-16 days; eyes open at 1 week; feathers develop within 10 days; young leave the nest at 16-24 days

redators: hawk, raccoon

ligration: migrates to Mexico and Central America

escription: The Tree Swallow is greenish blue with white dersides and a deeply forked tail.

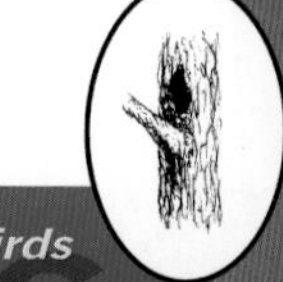

DID YOU KNOW...? Wild Turkeys commonly form flocks of 6 or more birds and roost in trees each evening. In spring males perform elaborate courtship displays to attract females In 1782, it lost by a single vote to the Bald Eagle as th national bird. Wild Turkeys were found in Massachusetts i colonial days, but disappeared by 1850 due to habitat loss They were reintroduced in the 1970s and there are now 18,000-20,000 Wild Turkeys in the state.

Turkey, Wild
Meleagris gallopavo

Size: body 3-4' long; 5' wingspan; males weigh 16-25 lbs.; females weigh 9-11 lbs.

Habitat: open wooded areas, cleared fields and brushy grasslands

Range: throughout Massachusetts except Nantucket and Suffolk Counties

Food: acorns, beechnuts, fruit, seeds, buds and insects

Nesting: April to May

Nest: hens nest in a depression on the ground, usually a leaf-lined hollow in heavy brush

Eggs: average clutch 10-12; buff with tan markings; 1 brood per year

Young: hatch in 28 days; precocial (covered with feathers and able to feed themselves); able to fly at 3-4 weeks, but remain with the female for up to 4 months

edators: fox, bobcat and Great Horned Owl

igration: present year-round

scription: The Wild Turkey is a large dark brown and ck bird with fan tail. Males have wattles (fleshy growths t hang beneath the chin), spurs (bony spear-like projecıs on the back of each leg), a snood (a flap of skin that pes over the bill), and a hair-like chest beard. Females more drab. They are strong short-distance flyers.

DID YOU KNOW...? The American Woodcock is also know as the Timberdoodle and the Bog Sucker. It has large eyes an nearly full circle vision. Its bill has highly sensitive nerve enc ings that can detect the movement of earthworms beneath th soil. In spite of its short wings, the American Woodcock i capable of flight speeds of 13 mph.

Woodcock, American

Scolopax minor

Size: body 10-12" long; 8-10 oz.

Habitat: open wooded areas, wetlands and old fields

Range: throughout Massachusetts

Food: earthworms, grubs and insects

Nesting: April to May

Nest: ground nest; measures 4-5" across

Eggs: average clutch 4; buff-colored with brown specks; 1 brood per year

Young: hatch in 20-21 days; young are precocial (hatch covered with down and able to feed themselves); young reach adult size at 25 days and are able to fly; fully independent at 6-8 weeks

edators: fox, coyote and raccoon

igration: migrates to southern states

scription: The American Woodcock is a cinnamon-col-
ed bird with dark brown splotches and extensive barring.
pinkish legs, neck, tail and wings are short. It is most
ive at night and early in the morning; look for rectangu-
holes (⅛" wide) in the soil made by its probing bill.

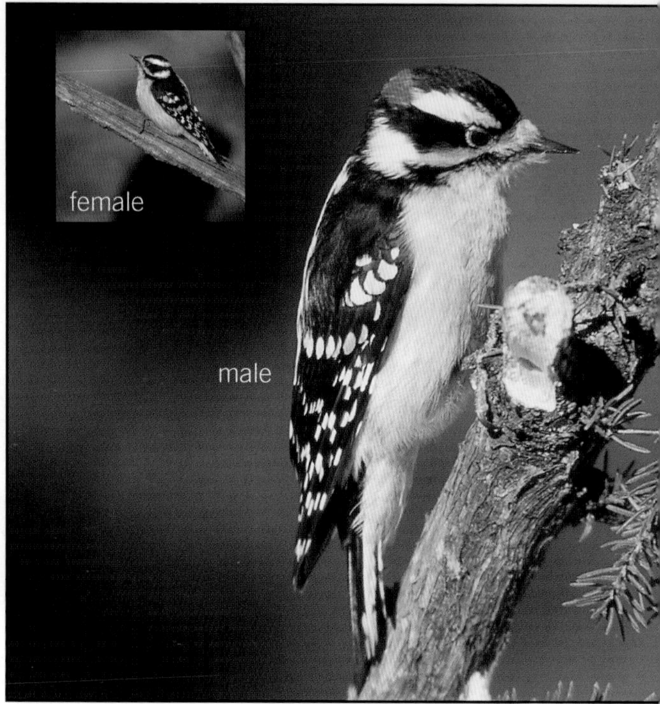

DID YOU KNOW...? The Downy Woodpecker has a chiseled bill it uses to tunnel into tree bark and a tongue specially adapted to spear insects. It uses its tail for support as it searches for food on tree trunks or excavates a nesting cavity. Each year, it excavates a new nesting site. Old sites become weatherproof nesting sites and burrows for other birds and wildlife.

Woodpecker, Downy

Picoides pubescens

Size: 5-6" long; 12" wingspan; 0.95 oz.

Habitat: wooded areas, parks and backyards

Range: throughout Massachusetts

Food: insects and insect larvae

Nesting: May to June

Nest: deep holes in trees, 1" wide

Eggs: average clutch 4-5; white; 1 brood per year; males and females tend eggs

Young: hatch in 11-12 days; young hatch blind and featherless; eyes open at 1 week; flight feathers appear at 13-20 days; young leave nest at 20-25 days, but adults continue to care for them for 3 weeks

redators: Northern Shrike, Cooper's Hawk and Sharp-shinned Hawk

ligration: present year-round

escription: The Downy Woodpecker is a distinctive black ıd white bird with white undersides and striped wings. The ale has a red patch on its head. Two forward-facing toes ıd two rear-facing toes help this bird to move up and down ee trunks.

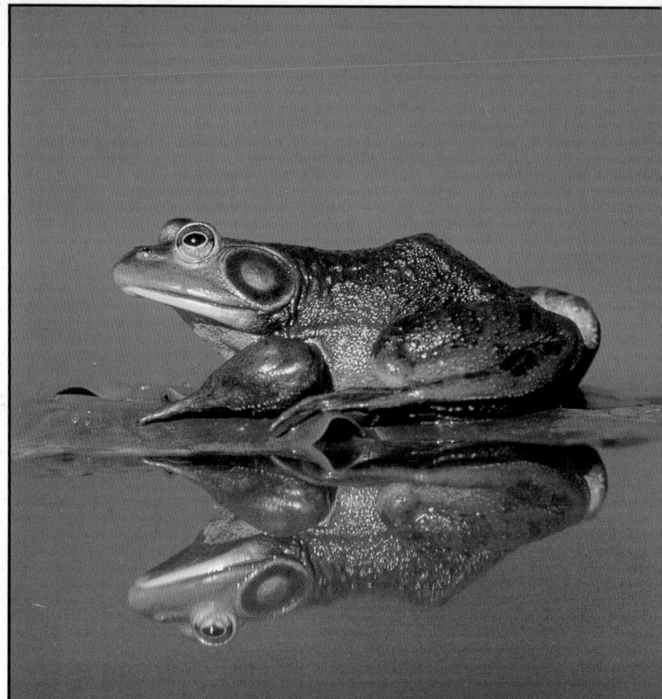

DID YOU KNOW...? The largest frog in North America, the bullfrog is capable of jumping 15 times its body length. It is one of the first frogs to go into hibernation each fall. It hibernates at the bottom of a lake or pond by burying itself in soft mud where it remains for several months before surfacing. It exchanges oxygen and water through its thin skin.

Bullfrog

Rana catesbeiana

Size: 3½ -8" long

Habitat: lakes, ponds and marshes with vegetation

Range: throughout Massachusetts except Dukes County

Food: fish, worms, insects, other frogs, snakes, mice, ducklings and young turtles; tadpoles (young frogs) feed on plant material (e.g. algae)

Mating: each spring the male attracts a mate with sound (jug-o-rum-more-rum) by inflating a balloon-like sac in its throat

Nest: no nest constructed

Eggs: the female lays up to 20,000 eggs in water in May to July; the male fertilizes the eggs immediately; the egg mass is covered in jell

Young: the eggs hatch into tadpoles in 5-20 days; the tadpoles live in water by breathing through gills; after 2 years, the tadpoles develop lungs and legs and are fully transformed into frogs

redators: birds, snakes, some mammals and other frogs

escription: Bullfrogs are green, black or brown with ack spots and white undersides. The male has exception-y large tympanums (eardrum areas).

DID YOU KNOW...? One of the most common frogs in the east, the familiar call of the spring peeper sounds much like the jingle of bells. A member of the tree frog family, the male spring peeper calls up to 4,000 times per hour by passing air from its lungs over its vocal cords to an elastic vocal sac that acts like a mini echo chamber. The call can be heard up to a mile away. Residents of Martha's Vineyard have nicknamed the spring peeper Pinkletinks. Its scientific name *crucifer* means crossbearer, referring to the X on its back.

nocturnal Zzz *hibernator*

Peeper, Spring

Pseudacris crucifer

Size: ½" long

Habitat: marshes, swamps, gardens and meadows near ponds

Range: throughout Massachusetts

Food: small insects and spiders

Mating: March to May

Nest: no nest constructed

Eggs: the female lays 800-1000 small, dark, jell-covered eggs in the water; the male fertilizes the eggs immediately; the eggs attach to aquatic plants and hatch in 7-10 days

Young: the young are called tadpoles or polliwogs; the tiny, fish-like tadpoles feed heavily on aquatic plants including algae; the young remain in the tadpole stage for 2-3 months during which time they transform quickly into land-dwellers; gills develop into lungs, legs sprout and the tail is absorbed; many tadpoles are eaten by fish, birds and other frogs

redators: otter, snake, bird, fish, large insects and other frogs

escription: The spring peeper is tan, brown and gray. It as a distinguishing X-shaped mark on its back. The male as a darker throat patch area.

DID YOU KNOW...? Like all amphibians, the American toad spends part of its life in water and part of its life on land. It is a member of the Anuran Order, meaning tailless. It has several defenses against predators including playing dead and burrowing into the soil. Its camouflage provides concealment and it can secrete a toxic white fluid that tastes awful and makes some animals sick. The American toad uses its long, sticky tongue to catch its prey. Contrary to popular myth, people do not get warts from toads.

nocturnal *crepuscular* Zzz *hibernator*

Toad, American

Bufo americanus

Size: 2-5" in length

Habitat: woodlands, ponds, lakes, grassy areas and gardens near water

Range: throughout Massachusetts except Nantucket

Food: flying and crawling insects, snails, worms and other frogs; young eat plant material

Mating: mid-March to mid-April; breeds in water

Nest: no nest constructed

Eggs: female lays thousands of jell-covered eggs in the water; male fertilizes the eggs immediately

Young: the young, called tadpoles or polliwogs, hatch within 7-14 days; the tadpoles live in water by breathing through gills and are roughly the size of a penny; they feed heavily on aquatic plants including algae; the tadpoles develop lungs and legs and transform into land-dwellers in 5-10 weeks

redators: fish, snake, bird, fox, muskrat and raccoon

escription: The American toad is usually brown or gray th dark spots and a light stripe down the center of its ck. Its undersides are cream colored. Its skin is covered th bumps. The male has a dark throat.

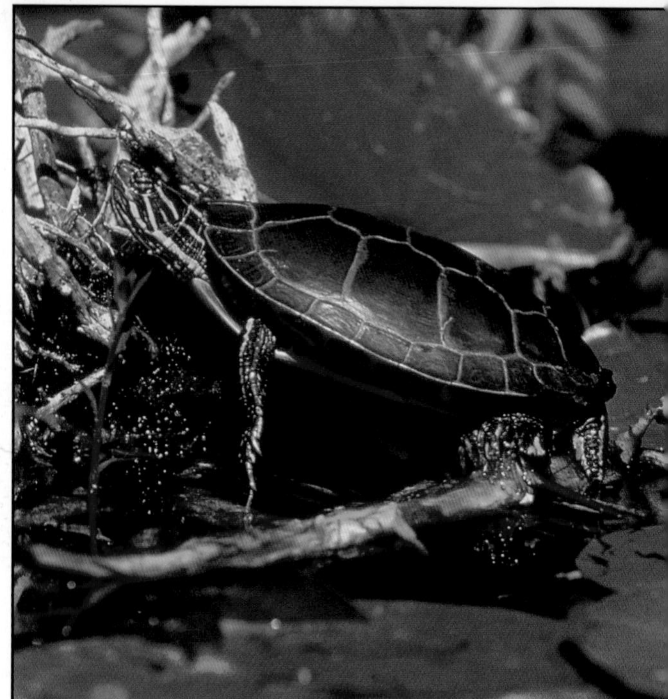

DID YOU KNOW...? North America is home to 56 species of turtles. Most turtles have hard shells made of keratin, similar to our fingernails. The painted turtle is the most common turtle in North America. It can be seen sunbathing in groups on logs and rocks at the water's edge. Like all reptiles, the painted turtle is cold-blooded, which means its body temperature is dependent on its surroundings. It spends the cold winter months buried in the soft mud of a pond or lake. The temperature of the nest determines the sex of the hatchlings.

TURTLE, PAINTED

Chrysemys picta

Size: 4-10" shell length

Habitat: lakes, ponds, marshes, slow-moving streams and rivers

Range: throughout Massachusetts

Food: water plants, insects, snails, tadpoles, crayfish, worms, small fish and carrion (remains of dead animals)

Mating: March and June

Nest: the female leaves the water to dig a nest-like hole, usually in sandy soil along beaches and roadsides; the eggs are buried and left

Eggs: average clutch 5-6; 1-2 clutches per year

Young: hatch in 60-80 days depending on temperature (late hatchlings may overwinter in the nest); the young are about the size of a quarter; immediately upon hatching the young head for the safety of nearby water where they feed on aquatic plants and insects

'redators: raccoon, fox and skunk prey on young

escription: The painted turtle is named for its brightly olored lower shell (plastron). The smooth, flat, oval-shaped pper shell (carapace) is olive-green and edged with red. Its ead, limbs and tail are marked with red and yellow. It has ebbed feet that are helpful for swimming. The female is enerally larger than the male.

DID YOU KNOW...? The snapping turtle, one of the largest turtles in North America, is a very aggressive predator. It often buries itself in mud with only its nostrils and eyes showing as it waits patiently to ambush its unsuspecting prey. The average life span of the snapping turtle is 30-40 years. It is commonly used in soups and stews. The heaviest recorded snapping turtle ever caught came from Massachusetts and weighed 76½ pounds.

Turtle, Snapping

Chelydra serpentina

Size: 8-20" shell length; average 8-35 lbs.; turtles weighing 40-80 lbs. are unusual

Habitat: lakes, ponds, rivers, streams and marshes

Range: throughout Massachusetts

Food: carrion (remains of dead animals), fish, birds, muskrats, snakes, frogs, aquatic plants, insects and other turtles

Mating: April to November

Nest: the female digs a deep hole in sandy soil, sometimes far from water; the eggs are buried and left

Eggs: average clutch size 25-35; white

Young: hatch in 80-90 days depending on temperature (late hatchlings may overwinter in nest); they are about the size of a quarter and immediately head for the safety of water; the young eat aquatic plants and insects

redators: fox, raccoon and skunk take eggs; mink, heron, raccoon and crow take young

escription: The snapping turtle is tan, brown, black or ve-gray. Its upper shell (carapace) has three keels or ges that may wear down with age. Its lower shell (plas-on) is significantly smaller. It has a long tail with pointed ges and its limbs are yellowish in color.

Lifelist

Place a check by critter you've seen, whether in your bac
yard, on a camping trip or at the zoo.

Mammals

- ☐ Bat, Little Brown
  Location: ______________________ Date: ______
  Comments: ______________________________
- ☐ Bear, Black
  Location: ______________________ Date: ______
  Comments: ______________________________
- ☐ Beaver
  Location: ______________________ Date: ______
  Comments: ______________________________
- ☐ Bobcat
  Location: ______________________ Date: ______
  Comments: ______________________________
- ☐ Chipmunk, Eastern
  Location: ______________________ Date: ______
  Comments: ______________________________
- ☐ Cottontail, Eastern
  Location: ______________________ Date: ______
  Comments: ______________________________
- ☐ Coyote, Eastern
  Location: ______________________ Date: ______
  Comments: ______________________________
- ☐ Deer, White-tailed
  Location: ______________________ Date: ______
  Comments: ______________________________

- ❑ Fisher
  Location: ______________________ Date: _______
  Comments: ______________________________
- ❑ Fox, Red
  Location: ______________________ Date: _______
  Comments: ______________________________
- ❑ Mink
  Location: ______________________ Date: _______
  Comments: ______________________________
- ❑ Moose
  Location: ______________________ Date: _______
  Comments: ______________________________
- ❑ Muskrat
  Location: ______________________ Date: _______
  Comments: ______________________________
- ❑ Opossum, Virginia
  Location: ______________________ Date: _______
  Comments: ______________________________
- ❑ Otter, River
  Location: ______________________ Date: _______
  Comments: ______________________________
- ❑ Porcupine
  Location: ______________________ Date: _______
  Comments: ______________________________
- ❑ Raccoon
  Location: ______________________ Date: _______
  Comments: ______________________________
- ❑ Skunk, Striped
  Location: ______________________ Date: _______
  Comments: ______________________________

☐ Squirrel, Eastern Gray
Location: ______________________ Date: ______
Comments: ______________________________

☐ Woodchuck
Location: ______________________ Date: ______
Comments: ______________________________

Birds

☐ Blackbird, Red-winged
Location: ______________________ Date: ______
Comments: ______________________________

☐ Bluebird, Eastern
Location: ______________________ Date: ______
Comments: ______________________________

☐ Cardinal, Northern
Location: ______________________ Date: ______
Comments: ______________________________

☐ Chickadee, Black-capped
Location: ______________________ Date: ______
Comments: ______________________________

☐ Crow, American
Location: ______________________ Date: ______
Comments: ______________________________

☐ Dove, Mourning
Location: ______________________ Date: ______
Comments: ______________________________

☐ Dove, Rock
Location: ______________________ Date: ______
Comments: ______________________________

- ☐ Duck, Wood
  Location: ______________________ Date: ________
  Comments: ______________________________
- ☐ Eagle, Bald
  Location: ______________________ Date: ________
  Comments: ______________________________
- ☐ Falcon, Peregrine
  Location: ______________________ Date: ________
  Comments: ______________________________
- ☐ Goose, Canada
  Location: ______________________ Date: ________
  Comments: ______________________________
- ☐ Grouse, Ruffed
  Location: ______________________ Date: ________
  Comments: ______________________________
- ☐ Gull, Herring
  Location: ______________________ Date: ________
  Comments: ______________________________
- ☐ Hawk, Red-tailed
  Location: ______________________ Date: ________
  Comments: ______________________________
- ☐ Heron, Great Blue
  Location: ______________________ Date: ________
  Comments: ______________________________
- ☐ Hummingbird, Ruby-throated
  Location: ______________________ Date: ________
  Comments: ______________________________
- ☐ Jay, Blue
  Location: ______________________ Date: ________
  Comments: ______________________________

- ☐ Loon, Common
  Location: ______________________ Date: ______
  Comments: ______________________
- ☐ Mallard
  Location: ______________________ Date: ______
  Comments: ______________________
- ☐ Owl, Great Horned
  Location: ______________________ Date: ______
  Comments: ______________________
- ☐ Robin, American
  Location: ______________________ Date: ______
  Comments: ______________________
- ☐ Swallow, Tree
  Location: ______________________ Date: ______
  Comments: ______________________
- ☐ Turkey, Wild
  Location: ______________________ Date: ______
  Comments: ______________________
- ☐ Woodcock, American
  Location: ______________________ Date: ______
  Comments: ______________________
- ☐ Woodpecker, Downy
  Location: ______________________ Date: ______
  Comments: ______________________

Other Critters

- ☐ Bullfrog
  Location: ______________________ Date: ______
  Comments: ______________________

☐ Peeper, Spring
Location: ______________________________ Date: _______
Comments: ____

☐ Toad, American
Location: ______________________________ Date: _______
Comments: ____

☐ Turtle, Painted
Location: ______________________________ Date: _______
Comments: ____

☐ Turtle, Snapping
Location: ______________________________ Date: _______
Comments: ____

Wild Words

A

Adaptation: a particular characteristic developed by a plant or a mal that makes it better suited to its environment.

Amphibians: cold-blooded, smooth-skinned vertebrates that spe part of their life on land and part of their life in the water inclu ing frogs, toads, newts and salamanders.

Anthropomorphism: attributing human characteristics to animals

Antler: bony projections grown and shed each year by members the deer family, typically males. Antlers are used in courts rivalries between competing males.

B

Behavior: the way in which an animal responds to its environme

Brood: (noun) the offspring of birds hatched at one time; (verb) hatch, protect and warm the young, usually done instinctively the female.

Browse: (noun) portions of woody plants including twigs, sho and leaves used as food by animals such as deer; (verb) to parts of woody plants.

Brumation: a period of winter dormancy brought on by droppi temperatures during which a reptile or amphibian's bo processes are slowed down and they become immobile.

Buck: a male deer, goat, pronghorn or rabbit.

Bull: a male moose, elk or bison.

Burrow: (noun) a hole, tunnel or underground den excavated by animal for shelter or refuge; (verb) to dig underground.

C

Camouflage: a protective adaptation that enables an animal to d guise itself or blend with its surroundings.

rnivore: an animal that eats other animals; a meat eater.

rrion: the body of a dead animal in the natural state of decay, which serves as a food source for other animals.

tch: a nest of eggs.

ld-blooded (ectothermic): an animal whose body temperature is dependent upon and varies with the temperature of its environment (e.g., fish, amphibians and reptiles).

mmunication: sound, scent or behavior recognized by members of the same species.

mpetition: different species of animals that use the same source for food or shelter.

nservation: the care, wise use and management of a resource.

nsumer: an animal that gets its food from producers (plants).

urtship: a behavior or series of actions an animal displays to indicate to the opposite sex that it is ready to mate in order to reproduce.

ver: naturally-occurring sheltered areas that provide concealment and shelter for wildlife, such as a dead tree, fallen log, rock outcrops, dense areas of brush or trees.

w: a female moose, wapiti (elk) or bison.

epuscular: active in twilight at dawn and dusk.

urnal: active during the day.

e: a female deer, pronghorn or rabbit.

wn: a layer of soft, fine feathers that provides insulation.

Drake: a male duck.

E

Ecology: the study of the relationships between living things a the environments in which they live.

Ecosystem: an interacting system of plants, animals, soil and mactic conditions in a self-contained environment (e.g., po marsh, swamp, lake or stream).

Endangered: a species in danger of becoming extinct due to dec ing population numbers.

Environment: the entire surroundings of an organism (plant or a mal) or group of organisms.

Estuary: area where fresh water and salt water meet.

Ethics: principles of good conduct; a sense of right and wrong.

Exotic: a foreign species introduced to an area from another reg or ecosystem. Exotic species are considered undesirable as th compete with native species for habitat and food.

Extinct: a species that no longer exists or has died out.

F

Fledgling: young birds learning to fly.

Food chain: plants and animals linked together as sources a consumers of food; typically an organism higher in the fc chain eats one lower in the food chain, so the health of one dependent on the health of another.

Food web: the many possible feeding relationships found withi given ecosystem.

Forage: (noun) plant material such as grasses, ferns, shrubs a the leaves and twigs of trees; (verb) to eat plant material.

ıme species: wildlife that can be hunted or trapped according to legal seasons and limits.

station: length of pregnancy.

abitat enhancement: the development and improvement of habitat (including sources of food, water, cover and space) for the benefit of fish or wildlife.

abitat: the local environment in which an animal lives. Components include food, water, cover (shelter) and space.

en: a female pheasant, duck, quail or turkey.

erbivore: an animal that eats only plant material.

bernation: a period of winter dormancy during which an animal's body processes slow dramatically, reducing the amount of energy required for survival. True hibernators' body processes slow nearly to a stop, and they require much less energy to survive. Deep sleepers' body processes do not slow as much, and they are more easily awakened.

ome range: the area over which an animal repeatedly travels in order to locate food, water and cover.

orn: hard protrusions that continuously grow on the head of certain mammals such as the bighorn sheep and bison. Horns are made of keratin, the same material that makes fingernails.

cubate: to warm eggs (usually bird eggs) with body heat so they develop and hatch. Females typically incubate the eggs.

Introduced species: a plant or animal brought from another regic often another continent, either intentionally or by accident; int duced species can have positive or negative effects on the nat species. Also referred to as "exotic" or "non-native," especia when the result is negative.

Invertebrates: animals without backbones, including insec earthworms and jellyfish.

J-L

Land ethic: deliberate, thoughtful and responsible consideration the natural landscape and natural resources, including wildli fossil fuels, soil, water and timber.

Land management: the purposeful manipulation of land or habi by people to encourage wildlife populations to increas decrease or stabilize in number. In the case of wildlife, th involves managing food, water, cover and space to affect pop lation numbers.

M

Mammal: a warm-blooded animal that has fur or hair and produc milk to feed its young.

Migration: the seasonal movements of fish and wildlife from o area to another usually triggered by length of daylight hou Animals that move varying distances at irregular times depe dent upon weather and availability of food are partial migrato Animals that move to the same places at the same times eve year are complete migrators.

N

Native: an indigenous or naturally-occurring species of plant animal.

Natural resource: materials found in nature to which people ha assigned value such as timber, fresh water, wildlife and fos fuels (coal and oil).

:turnal: an animal that is active by night.

ıgame species: the majority of wildlife not hunted by humans ıcluding songbirds, raptors, reptiles and amphibians.

ırenewable resources: nonliving natural resources which, for all ractical purposes, cannot be replaced, including metallic minrals, such as gold and copper, and fossil fuels, such as coal nd oil.

nivore: an animal that eats both plants and animals (meat).

ortunist: an animal that can take advantage of any number of ood sources available.

romone: a chemical scent secreted as a means of communiation between members of the same species.

tosynthesis: the process by which plant cells convert light, vater and carbon dioxide into energy and nutrients while simulaneously releasing oxygen.

mage: the feathers of a bird.

lution: toxic (poisonous) substances deposited in the air, water r soil creating an unhealthy environment.

ulation: a collection of individuals of the same species in a iven area whose members can breed with one another.

dator: an animal that hunts and feeds on other animals (prey).

y: an animal hunted or killed for food by other animals (predators).

ducers: plants that obtain energy from the sun and produce ood through the process of photosynthesis.

R

ıge: the particular geographic region in which a species is found.

Raptor: a bird of prey including falcons, owls, eagles, hawks ospreys.

Recreation: an activity undertaken for enjoyment; entertainm often associated with natural resources (water, forests, rock mations) includes rock climbing, bird watching, fish canoeing and hunting.

Renewable natural resource: a natural resource that can be rep ished and harvested, including trees and wildlife.

Reptile: cold-blooded vertebrate animals that lay eggs (e snakes, lizards and turtles).

Riparian area: lands adjacent to streams, rivers, lakes and ot wetlands where the vegetation is influenced by the great a ability of water.

Roost: refers to a safe gathering place used by wildlife, usu birds and bats, for rest or sleep.

Rut: activity associated with breeding behavior.

S

Scat: refers to defecation, excrement or waste.

Scavenger: an animal that feeds on the remains of dead anim

Scrape: an area where concentrated amounts of urine are mi with mud to attract a mate or indicate territory.

Season: time of year when game species may be legally harvest

Sow: a female bear.

Species: a group of animals that have similar structure, comm ancestors and characteristics they maintain through breedir

Stewardship: responsible care of natural resources for future g erations.

king: the artificial propagation and introduction of game pecies into an area.

itory: the area an animal will defend, usually during breeding eason, against intruders of its own species.

atened: a classification for wildlife species whose population is great decline and approaching the "endangered" classifica-on.

/

ebrates: animals with a backbone, including fish, birds, mam-als, reptiles and amphibians.

Z

m-blooded (endothermic): an animal whose body temperature unrelated to its environment (e.g., mammals and birds).

an: (noun) young that no longer depend on an adult for food; verb) to withhold mother's milk from young and substitute other ourishment.

dlife: non-domesticated plants and animals (including mam-als, birds, fish, reptiles, insects and amphibians).

dlife agency: a state or federal organization responsible for anaging wildlife.

dlife management: a combination of techniques, scientific nowledge and technical skills used to protect, conserve and anage wildlife and habitat.

ter kill: the death of animals during winter resulting from lack f food and exposure to cold.

Wildlife Forever Projects in Massachusetts

- Purchased tracking transmitters to be used by wildlife biol gists with the Division of Fisheries and Wildlife for trackin black bears that had not been radio-collared.
- Purchased 115 acres of land near Royalston to protect a important riparian corridor, including a coldwater stream, we lands and upland habitat. In addition to protecting valuab wildlife habitat, this purchase continues to provide excelle recreational opportunities for outdoor enthusiasts.
- Purchased and dedicated 460 acres of land to th Massachusetts Westboro Biodiversity Initiative, helping to cr ate the largest and longest suburban wildlife corridor in th New England region.
- Removed a dam that was constructed in 1910 on th Housatonic River and was no longer in use. The removal the dam improved native trout and coldwater fish habitat.
- Restored and enhanced 30 acres of ditched and altered sa marsh in Essex County.

RULER

Find tracks? Use this guide to measure them.

entimeters

1 2 3 4 5 6 7 8 9

inches

0 1 2 3 4 5